To Tyler,

Go
to your dr[eam]
of building a com[munity]
of visionaries around
[you]!

Praise For
PURE THOUGHTS for PURE RESULTS

"*Pure Thoughts for Pure Results* helps you understand how much life has to offer, if we understand the process by which we create our life experience. When you see how much this book help maximize your experience of life you won't be able to keep it to yourself! You'll want to share it with everyone you know!"

–Sharon Lechter, New York Times bestselling author of Rich Dad Poor Dad and Think and Grow Rich – Three Feet from Gold; Member of the President's Advisory Council on Financial Literacy

"After I read *Pure Thoughts for Pure Results,* I thought about the great value of having a book like this that acts as a handbook for living life. It made me ponder about much time and grief I would have saved if this book had been available to me when I was starting my adult life and my career. Don't go another day without reading this great guide to great living!"

–Judge Douglas Bench, Founder of Science for Success Systems

"In *Pure Thoughts for Pure Results,* Crystal offers insights that are profound. With the turn of each page, you will find a pure treasure. I am always looking for ways to understand life and live it better, so I can enthusiastically recommend the book to any and all."

–Bill Froehlich, Producer, Writer, Director, - MacGyver, Hart to Hart, The Outer Limits.

"If you want to understand how to live the life you want more with less effort and more ease and joy, don't just read this book but carry it with you everywhere! *Pure Thoughts for Pure Results* is my new reference guide for living!"

–Candace Sandy, Communications Director for Congressman Gregory W. Meeks, National Bestselling Author and Co-Publisher of Souls of Sisters Book, an imprint of Kensington Publishing Corp.

"*Pure Thoughts for Pure Results* is pure magic. Not another self-help book but a step-by-step guide to help you maximize your journey of life through both the heart and the mind. Once you read this book you'll understand how to stay out of "Messy Thinking" forever!"

–Andy Andrews, Inspirational Speaker and New York Times Bestselling author of The Traveler's Gift

Pure Thoughts for Pure Results

How **Messy Thinking** Can Make Or Break Your Life

CRYSTAL DWYER

CrystalVision Publishing
Scottsdale, Arizona

The publisher and author of this material make no medical
or psychological claims or any other explicit claims for its use. This
material is not intended to treat, diagnose, advise about, or cure any
illness. If you need medical attention or
psychological therapy, please consult with your
medical practitioner or psychologist.

Copyright © 2008 by Crystal Dwyer.
All rights reserved.

No part of this book may be reproduced or transmitted in any form
or by any means, electronic or mechanical,
including photocopying, recording, or by information
storage and retrieval systems, without the
written permission of the author and publisher.

ISBN: 1-4392-1265-1
ISBN-13: 9781439212653

Visit www.booksurge.com to order additional copies.

*To Preston, Shannon, and Kelly,
three shining stars who always light up my life*

Contents

Forward — *xi*
Acknowledgments — *xiii*
Introduction — *xv*

Part One Your Mind Makeover Framework

Chapter 1	Whose Life Are You Really Living?	1
Chapter 2	You Thought You Were Your Thoughts	17
Chapter 3	Anatomy of a Thought	43
Chapter 4	History Lesson: Studying Your Family's Belief/Behavior Patterns	55
Chapter 5	Emotions: Your Mind/Body Connection	71

Part Two The Seven Pillars of Transformation

Chapter 6	The First Pillar: Self-Honesty	93
Chapter 7	The Second Pillar: Observation	107
Chapter 8	The Third Pillar: Choice	125
Chapter 9	The Fourth Pillar: Responsibility	145
Chapter 10	The Fifth Pillar: Imagination	161
Chapter 11	The Sixth Pillar: Action	181
Chapter 12	The Seventh Pillar: Silence	195

Part Three Your New Creation Begins

| Chapter 13 | Karma: The Reckoning Force of All Intention | 215 |
| Chapter 14 | Quantum Leaps: Implementing the Pillars for Massive Change | 223 |

Recommended Resources	239
Notes	249
About the Author	255

Foreword

by Mark Victor Hansen

Thinking is everything! Everything comes from thinking. Ancient wisdom says: "Mind is all." And "Thoughts are things."

My dear friend and colleague, Crystal Dwyer, has written a book elucidating that ancient wisdom in a practical step-by-step guide to rising up and transcending these challenging times. *Pure Thoughts for Pure Results* is the perfect book to nurture us into making the shift to clear thinking.

God's *thought* forms created the Universe. You and I were given the power of conscious thought to create our respective and individual universe. If you do "messy thinking," obviously, you get to live in a "messy universe."

As you think right, you will talk right, act right and get the right results. Right thinking over time compounds to a right livelihood, right living, right lifestyle and all of the right experiences which lead to greatness.

Through her personal challenges and triumphs and her depth of experience in coaching and guiding others, Crystal has perfected the art of higher manifestation through higher thinking and has earned the right to write about, teach and lead great seminars on right thinking and right results, right now! In this life-changing book, she clearly and brilliantly gives you the step-by-step plan to go from messy thinking to magnificent thinking. This reading experience guides you to your own mastery of *Pure Thoughts for Pure Results*.

I have observed my friend Crystal. She has done it and you can too. Her life, lifestyle, family, friends, fortune, and future are the result of great right thinking that keeps getting ever better results. Crystal wants the same or more for you. That's why she wrote this important, make-a-difference book to help you make all good things happen in your life in the sweet *now*.

Drink deeply of her wisdom, apply it, and move from messy to magnificent thinking. Thus, you will create a life worthy of who you really are.

Through the reading of this book, you will become empowered by the insights, tools, and techniques you need to employ your full talents and to manifest your absolute potential… making all your dreams, hopes, desires bloom from your bountiful imagination.

Acknowledgments

First, I would like to acknowledge my mother and father, who gave me life and always loved me. You both provided the anchor for all of this work to go forward. I am also grateful to my amazing children whose spirit, determination, and curiosity have caused me to grow in ways that only they could have brought about. My love for them is a deep well from which I will always drink in joy, serenity, and purpose. Thanks also to Mike, for hanging in there and supporting me even when it was hard to see why. And thanks to my other parents, Marguerite and Frank, whose love and presence has been a constant stabilizer.

I would like to express my gratitude to my beautiful clients who put their vulnerability on the line and allow me to learn and grow with them, as well as to the delightful, God-appointed cast of characters called my brothers and sisters. I love beyond words each one in this little clan.

Janet, Dorothy, Kathy, Karen, Judy, Evie, Daune, Ann, Leslie, and Kim, my first and best fans—life wouldn't be complete without you, my amazing group of women friends who are always there to laugh with, cry with, and cheer one another on.

Thank you to my amazing editor, Stephanie Gunning. How blessed I have been to work with this woman who has put so much care into this work that she has become an invaluable partner.

I am also grateful to my special mentors and teachers, Deepak Chopra, M.D., David Simon, M.D., Linda Bennett, K.C. Miller, Carol Tuttle, Gary Craig and Mark Victor Hansen, all of whom have left their indelible mark on the work that I do.

A big thanks to Jason Hendricks, Don Kupper, Sam Ray, and Beverly Bowen for keeping things going on the technical side and working out our glitches at a moment's notice. I couldn't have pulled this book off without each of you. And if there is anyone I forgot to mention who feels I should have…you are right, and please forgive me for forgetting to in my eagerness to finish this project.

Finally, I am thankful to God, the Source of all of it.

Introduction

"Nobody can go back and start a new beginning, but anyone can start today and make a new ending."
—Maria Robinson

The inspiration for this book came to me one day as I was driving from the beautiful red rocks of Sedona, Arizona, back to the valley of Metro Phoenix where I live. Sedona has become a sacred haven for me, for the past six or seven years. I always seem to experience an abundance of inspiration and clarity while spending time there.

Thus inspired, I was winding down the open road looking at the valley below and reflecting on how much I love my life and how blessed I am. I thought about the many people I know and with whom I work, who really struggle with life and don't *love* their lives as much as I do. It suddenly dawned on me what a travesty it is for anyone *not* to love life and be living it to the fullest. Life is a gift to be loved.

Then I thought, "My life has not been easy. In fact, it's been challenging and downright brutal at times. How can I be so happy when so many people aren't?"

I began to ask myself questions that would ultimately become the basis for this book, such as:

- "What specific steps did I take to get where I am today?"
- "What strategies and tools have I developed that got me to this point?"
- "How was I able to transcend tremendous challenges and to keep moving toward the life of my dreams that I now live?"

The more questions I asked, the more clearly I realized that I *do* live by a specific set of principles; ones that have allowed me to keep clearing the hurdles in my life and transcending to a higher level of happiness and achievement each time. An idea was born. If I could write a book that would allow *anyone* to apply the same principles and tools that I had used, in *their* own lives, perhaps the world would be blessed with happier, more successful people.

The work I do, as a life coach and hypnotherapist, allows me the privilege of guiding people from where they are in their lives to where they want to be. Often, when I take on a new client, our starting point on the path toward their dreams and greatest destiny is a place laden with dissatisfaction, confusion, or pain. From this place, I am able to assist my clients through the process of illuminating the source of their discontent, decoding the thought patterns and habits that have kept them locked in pain or confusion, and finally forming a new strategy for moving joyfully down a new path.

I knew my book, *Pure Thoughts for Pure Results,* needed to start out by helping people understand what really is going on in their physical brains, and the emotional/mental connections happening inside of them, so they would understand how those patterns constantly contribute to the creation of their lives. People got really excited about the blockbuster movie *The Secret w*hen it first came out in 2006. The law of attraction truly seemed like the key to success and happiness… and it is a key. But it's not the whole picture of how we create our lives with our thoughts. Without understanding the subconscious emotional and thought patterns that are continually moving through the mind and the body, people will keep attracting what they don't want.

Some people are disenchanted with the law of attraction and say it doesn't work for them. It actually *is* working for them, flawlessly. What these people aren't yet in touch with is how the *messy thinking* that's hiding below the surface in their minds and in their cells is running their lives. The program I've created, that is the basis of this book, teaches people how to break into these subconscious thought patterns and essentially to re-wire themselves. I have become passionate about sharing this information.

If you understand how all parts of the creative "you" work, nothing in life can shut you down. You will be truly empowered to transcend any adversity and to create something better from it. I know this is true because I've been there. I believe God loaded my life with challenges, heartaches, and turmoil from a young age, so that I would have to learn to step up and find a way back to happiness and peace.

I can honestly say, I have been through the Valley of the Shadow of Death and out the other side enough times to have developed a certain expertise on how it is done. Both the victories and the struggles I have experienced in my life have led me on a quest to discover how the workings of the mind control the experience of our lives, from the physiological, to the emotional level, to the highest spiritual level of quantum creation.

When I was in the eighth grade, the IRS prosecuted my father. He lost his case. After the decision that he had paid insufficient taxes, a judge sentenced Dad to a year in Lompoc, a minimum-security penitentiary. He would be leaving his wife, nine children, and a law practice behind. My previously normal life seemed suddenly to spin out of my control. The range of emotions I felt included shame, worry, anger, and a cold fear of what was happening to our family and the existence I'd always known.

A few years later, still shaken and wounded from my dad's year-long absence... I was 15 when my parents underwent a nasty divorce. My eight siblings and I found it hard to maintain our identities in the wake of our parents' battles. In only a few short years the ground on which we had all solidly stood gave way, and we were each flailing to regain our footing. In my case, I came to the conclusion that high school had nothing more to offer me, so I accelerated my curriculum. I graduated at the end of my junior year, at age 16. Three months later in an attempt to rebound from my pain and uncertainty, I married myself off to the first boy who swore he couldn't live without me.

Just one week after my seventeenth birthday, I wed a 22-year-old kid who had no more business getting married than I did. We were both too young and immature to succeed. Subsequently, three and a half years later I found myself trying to work through my own divorce, with a two-year old baby boy on my hip, residing in a new city where I had no job, no friends or family around me, and no real plan of what to do next. I was too proud to ask for help from my parents. The only option I left myself was to figure it out alone. At one point, I applied for food stamps so I could buy diapers and food. But when I stood in the grocery line the first time I used them, I felt sick inside. Something inside of me was repulsed by the idea of accepting help because I equated it with incompetence. I became determined to support myself. There was a part of me that couldn't accept the situation I was in. I knew that I was capable of earning money and paying my bills on my own. I made a vow to myself, in that moment, that I would finish the food stamps I had for the month and never reapply. I knew that if I would just dig deeper inside myself, I would find the resources to make my life happen the way I wanted it to. I was 21 by then, and ready to step into my adulthood and be in charge of my life.

The next day, I scanned the job ads again and called three temporary service agencies. I registered with all of them, so that I would have a constant stream of options for jobs. I did everything from clerical work and receptionist work to setting up display booths at malls. I was learning a lot about many different kinds of businesses, working with many different kinds of people, and enjoying the variety. I would be assigned to some jobs for up to several months and some for only a few days. I was happy to be able to pay my bills, buy food, take good care of my little boy, and still have a little fun.

During this time period, several people approached me to see if I would consider doing some modeling. I decided I had nothing to lose so I investigated various agencies, made appointments to meet them, and ended up signing a management contract with one of the top modeling agencies in my town. It didn't take long before I was hired as a model for some well-paying print ads and television commercials. Life began to get a bit easier for my little guy and me once I had this new stream of income.

The money I made as a model allowed me to put myself through a training program and begin a career selling real estate. Right after I finished the program and got my real estate license, I started working for the top homebuilder in our valley. In a short time I was salesperson of the month. I was making great money, and enjoyed being in charge of my life for the first time. But although I felt empowered and capable, life still had a few more hard lessons for me.

Only two years after my divorce, I fell in love and remarried. The first year of my new marriage was anything but fun for me. I had a pronounced insecurity about men. I was honest enough with myself to realize the fear I carried that men were untrustworthy was due to my childhood feelings about my father. My husband was completely focused on his work. He also had a hard time connecting emotionally with me, which often left me feeling lonely in our marriage. In addition, I was constantly fighting my fear of becoming too dependent on my husband and losing the identity I had worked so hard to create.

There were so many times I felt emotionally distraught. But rather than throw in the towel, I was determined to rise above the turmoil I felt inside, and find a way to create pockets of happiness wherever I could. Over the ensuing years, we had two daughters who we raised side-by-side with my son.

I poured myself into the role of being a super-mom; taking classes to finish my college degree and building and decorating the houses my husband and I were adding to our real estate portfolio, at the same time I was running our household. Being productive and constantly busy provided me with a distraction from the emptiness I often felt.

Over the next thirteen years, many of the happy times my husband and I had together were marred by an ongoing battle with my first husband, over the custody of my son. It seemed that neither he nor my second husband was willing to give up on the idea of having absolute control over my son's life. My son and

I were continually caught in a vice grip of two opposing masculine forces pushing to get their own way at any cost. This turmoil abruptly ended, when my son ran away to live with his father in Utah. My heart was torn. Although I wanted my son to come home, I honored his choice to leave and allowed him to finish high school there. My husband was not as forgiving as I was.

During the next six years, my son struggled with depression. His feelings of being rejected by his stepdad led him to limit his direct communication with me—a practice his father encouraged. I felt constant frustration and powerless to change the tone of our relationship or to help him; now that he was living in a different state. My husband and I and our two younger daughters lived in Arizona. Throughout those years away from me, my son made choices that led him through some tough, scary experiences. A silver lining in this dark cloud was my son's ultimate realization that he could count on my love and support. I look back with gratitude that when he opened up communication with me again, the tools and knowledge I had developed, as a hypnotherapist, enabled me to help him overcome problems that easily could have become perpetual stumbling blocks.

My personal journey, over the years, led me to pursue an education in several healing modalities that provided me knowledge of how the mind works, at all levels of consciousness. These include neuro-linguistic programming (NLP), hypnotherapy, emotional freedom technique (EFT), meditation, and life coaching. I've been blessed to study under many wise masters and teachers from each of whom I've gained tremendous insight, truth, and value. My desire, both for myself and for the people I love, to be able to see their greatness and learn to operate from that state of consciousness has kept me searching for insights that could provide enlightenment in my life or theirs.

My education in these areas has been enormously helpful in navigating through other difficult family challenges as they've come up in our lives. My husband and I worked hard for many years to overcome personal issues that have come between us, and threats to our children's well-being. At age 12, our youngest daughter developed a life-threatening eating disorder; a frightening and devastating situation for any family to go through. But once again, by reaching an understanding of how each of us carried thought and emotional programming that had contributed to the development of her disorder, we got to the core of the problem and then everyone in the family, especially my daughter, had to step up to their responsibility to help her heal.

We learned that an eating disorder has no single origin, but is instead, an intricate jigsaw puzzle. When the final piece snaps into place you get the full picture that has been created by so many little parts. As painful as the ordeal was for her and for all of us, it caused her to evolve into a remarkably strong, focused, and compassionate young woman. She turned her life around, began to love and honor herself again, and even became involved in mentoring other teenage girls with eating disorders.

When we first had to face this issue that was so near to our hearts, it would have been easy to collapse into the fears that we felt and wonder if we could ever really solve this. Fortunately, we were able to learn the tools, and we were willing to do the inner work that was required to get through it and move forward in a healthier way.

At some point in our lives, each of us will be faced with issues that we feel helpless to resolve let alone go forward to create something better. When we can no longer tolerate the way our lives look or feel, or the way *we* look or feel, it is time for a massive *makeover of the mind.* In the process of any transformation, we must start with the mind because it is the master control center of human existence. The mind provides the vehicle through which our experiences are interpreted and processed, and it is the avenue through which our soul ultimately can express itself on the earthly plane we reside in.

The concept of mind encompasses not only what is happening within the brain but also consciousness, separate from the physical organ. So when I refer to a "mind makeover," I am talking about much more than the mental processes, alone. I am speaking of the consciousness that rests within the brain and also goes beyond our physical boundaries to participate in a constant exchange of knowledge, wisdom, and presence.

By the time I was almost finished writing this book, I had written over 100 titles. Then one day as I was focused on something completely different; the current title literally dropped into my head. *Pure Thoughts for Pure Results* describes the ultimate state of thinking. Thinking done with purity and clarity, devoid of the messy clutter that inhabits most of our minds and hinders our most powerfully creative thinking.

The work I do has allowed me to facilitate and witness miraculous makeovers in people's lives. I've seen people who have been haunted with crushing depression their entire lives become completely depression-free. I've seen people who've suffered from debilitating panic and fear learn to release their fears, and to trust the process of life as it unfolds. I've nurtured and challenged people, who have held excessive weight as part of their identity for much of their lives, to break free and live healthy, fit lives. I've also assisted those who were controlled by a smoking addiction, or a drug addiction that might have eventually killed them, in becoming addiction-free, forever.

I've coached people who felt like they had lost themselves, when an intimate relationship ended, to find a much better version of who they are and to move on to a better life than they had previously imagined. I have assisted people in making over their lives and transforming themselves in countless ways they had doubted were possible. Every one of these miraculous life changes came about through *a makeover of the mind*.

Acting as guide, witness, and seeker of truth, I learn as much from my clients as they learn from me. I participate, regularly, in interactions that give me such reverence for the human spirit and its unfailing ability to resurrect itself again and again. My personal journey of life, through both the joyful and the devastating has led me to a special place that I wish to share with you in this book. It is my hope that it will open new doors for you, and help you to see the path behind you and before you a little more clearly.

PART ONE

Your Mind Makeover Framework

✺

In Part One, we will go through a detailed explanation of the different areas of life where *messy thinking* gets started. Think of this section as a primer to a mind makeover that you'll undergo using the techniques and philosophy described in Part Two. It provides a discussion of the origins of *messy thinking*. Our tendency to identify with our thoughts, our physiological brain structure, our thought/emotion chemistry, and our learned family dynamics all set a framework in place for our thinking, which often becomes *messy thinking*. All of these components create hidden programming that contributes to a whole picture of how we process our lives, and the results we get from our process.

After you read through these five chapters, you will begin to understand the foundations of your thinking, at the subconscious and conscious levels. You will start to understand why you've experienced some of the difficulties you have had in your thought processes. All of your patterns will start to make more sense. Based on that understanding, the mind makeover framework will prepare you to move forward to Part Two, and the implementation of the Seven Pillars of Transformation.

Chapter One
Whose Life Are You Really Living?

"It is not in the stars to hold our destiny but in ourselves."
—William Shakespeare

Whose life are you really living? It might seem like a silly question. Here you are immersed in your life. Stuff happens. You're trying to keep up with the daily grind plugging away to keep all the balls in the air, but sometimes fearful they all could come crashing down at any moment. At times, you might feel anxious, depressed, or overwhelmed. It may be that you struggle with weight issues or health issues. And then there are your relationships. Are your relationships full and alive or rather empty and unfulfilling? Do you enjoy loving, heartfelt, engaged connection with those you love or has love become about routine or convenience—or is love even non-existent in your life?

What about the issue of career and money? Do you consistently worry about career or money challenges? Are you approaching your means of earning a living with trepidation or enthusiasm? Even if your career is moving forward does it lack purpose and fulfillment for you?

In private moments of self-reflection, perhaps you find yourself wondering how you ended up here. But this is your life, right? Or is it? Did you ever stop to *really* think about the life you're living and take inventory? If you took some time to reflect on what your life is about, how it is unfolding, and what themes keep recurring as you move through the years, what would you come up with? What would life look like if you stood back and really examined it?

If you were totally honest with yourself, you might admit that the main issues that challenge you keep playing out again and again in different ways. The situation is different, the people involved may even be different, but the core issues seem to resurface over and over again in most of our lives only in a slightly different form. In what areas of your life does it seem as if you just keep missing the target?

As you go through this life inventory process are you able to challenge your current issues and believe things could be different, or have you accepted that this is how life *is*? Or that this is who you *are*? Do you believe that even if you resolve your current problems more will come up and you'll never really get ahead of them? For many people life seems predestined, as if they are at the mercy of forces outside of them and their control.

I'd like to ask you to take a few moments to do the following exercise as you begin your life transformation journey. It is most important not to filter your answers, but to let them flow. There is no right or wrong and any revelations or thoughts you come up with are meant only for you. This is *your* journey; so let's get started.

1. Am I living my ideal life? (Circle your answer). Yes No

2. In which areas do I feel the least fulfilled? (Rank each area from 1–10).

   Money/career _____   Relationships _____

   Health _____   Weight and Fitness _____

   Spirituality _____   Life Purpose/Contribution _____

3. Does my life feel out of my own control? (Circle your answer). Yes No

4. Do I sometimes feel like something is standing in the way of me living my ideal life? (Circle your answer). Yes No

5. Do I often feel powerless to change things? (Circle your answer). Yes No

6. At times does it seem that others have more control over the decisions I make than I do? (Circle your answer). Yes No

7. Do I feel powerful and resourceful enough, right now, if I wanted to change things? (Circle your answer). Yes No

8. How long have I felt this way about the questions above? (In your own words).

Now that you've answered the above questions, close your eyes for a moment and ask yourself, "What would my ideal life look like, feel like, *be like?*" Then, keeping your eyes closed listen for the answers. When you open your eyes write down all of the words that come to you that describe the life you just envisioned.

Once you get a vision of your ideal life through this visualization exercise… ask yourself if this life you envisioned is anything like the one you're living now, or if the life you just imagined is one that only other people get to live?

Can you even imagine the greatest challenges you've always experienced being absent from the picture? Are you able to form a mental picture of a life for yourself that includes robust health, vitality, and fitness? Can you actually see yourself free of destructive habits? Can you envision yourself in a passionate, fulfilling relationship with someone you love and worship? Can you capture a picture of yourself in a dynamic, successful career doing work you love to do: a job you embrace with enthusiasm each and every day?

I want you to think about your most amazing life vision and compare it to the life you are currently living. On a scale of 1 to 10, with 10 being your most amazing life where does the life you're living rank?

Do you believe you could really have the perfect life you imagined? If not, why? We all see and know other people who live amazing lives. Why is it that often it is easier to picture an ideal life for someone else but not for you? Robust health, vital physical fitness, freedom from self-defeating destructive habits, passionate relationships, and an exciting, fulfilling career... are those qualities of life ones that you could only imagine for someone else?

Stop Claiming a Life That's Not Yours

So if your life lacks the dynamic qualities that would be ideal for you whose life *are* you living? When you really stop to think about it... isn't it a mystery that so many people live a life that is so unlike the one they truly desire? Imagine what life would be like if you could solve that mystery. If you could truly zone in on the very things that hold you back and then change them.

I've written this book to help you do just that. To help you uncover what holds you back from your deepest desires. To help you dare to dream again. Your reading will take you through a discovery process that shows you how you can create a life that is *truly* yours. This process takes you on an evolutionary journey showing you that you *can* live a life that meets your greatest vision, standards, and ideals. It prepares you to claim a life that is of your own deliberate making. The good news is that in order to find the keys that unlock this mystery of life, you don't have to venture very far. In fact, all of the answers are inside of you *now*.

An Expedition to the Center of You

This process is a journey within. Think of it as an excavation project in which we dig deep below the surface of the conscious mind to uncover what lies in the layers of the subconscious. We sift through the years of accumulated programs, memories, beliefs, and attitudes. Once we expose what's within to the light of day, we can carefully decide which of those programs, memories, beliefs, and attitudes are serving our new life vision and which are not.

Then with me coaching you through the Seven Pillars of Transformation, you will have the ability to clear out anything that would be sabotaging your greatest success and dreams. Each chapter is designed to take you forward, with tools and techniques to reframe and build new patterns that will help facilitate great changes in the way you process, mold, and shape your life.

What Makes Us Give Up on Ourselves?

People are challenged every day with issues of every kind. In my practice as a life coach and hypnotherapist, I see many clients who are struggling with emotional, mental, and physical pain. I see people who feel the success they desire in their careers continues to elude them, and that maybe they just don't have what it takes to be successful. I see clients who believe, at the deepest level, that the money they want to earn is never achievable, and that being the best in their field is a distinction for others, not for them. I see people who have seriously given up on the idea that the loving, passionate relationship they desire is ever possible.

No matter what challenges come your way, what if you could feel completely certain that you have internal resources that would prevent you from *ever* considering giving up? What if you would always be able to look at the challenges you were confronted with and know that you not only would overcome them, but also that you would become stronger, happier, and more resourceful in doing so?

Something's Missing, But Why Can't You Figure Out What It Is?

When people struggle or feel unfulfilled, the common thread that runs through all of their experiences is the lack of connection they feel to the outcome they're getting in their lives. The people I see who are not satisfied with their lives are, without fail, *profoundly disconnected* from the results they are getting from their life experience. They feel life just happens. Bad things just keep sneaking into their reality popping up in unexpected places at unexpected times. Many people feel as though bad luck can rear its ugly head at any moment and render them powerless in their lives. To them, it is as if there is a force somewhere outside of them that randomly causes suffering, just because it can. People often live their entire lives hoping to stay one step ahead of the defeat, pain, or suffering that seems to keep chasing them.

The reason people fail to get their desired result is because they are not seeing *their own* creative role in their life experience. Whether or not we realize it, we are creating our reality and defining our experience, and the way we are doing it is through our thoughts. Our thoughts actually have formed (and will continue to form) our perception and our beliefs and, consequently, the actions we do or do not take which create our experience. This in turn creates the reality we call *our life*.

At this point, you might be saying, "No way! This can't be! If I were the one creating my life, I would definitely have created something better than this." Stay tuned. Read on. We are embarking on a journey, together, that will answer these questions and clear up any confusion or denial you might be experiencing.

The Genesis of the Thought Patterns Underlying Our Lives

Many of the thoughts and thought patterns that lock you into the same predictable outcomes in your life are happening at the subconscious level. Consciously, you are not even aware they are happening. The thought patterns that run your life began to form at the time of your birth. These patterns have become more established and reinforced, through every ensuing life experience and situation you have encountered, up to this very moment. Your own perceptions and thoughts that were processed (in different situations) created mental structures and patterns that were reshaped and modified only when you challenged them, and accepted or learned something new.

Challenging your established mental structures and patterns, and accepting and learning new ways to operate *now* will open the door to a whole new way of living… making way for the creation of a life you love living. The program in this book gives you the steps you need to make the changes happen.

So, if the experience called life has been largely shaped by your own perceptions and thoughts, do you like your life experience, so far? Are you enjoying the experience of life you are helping to create? If not are you willing to examine what you've created? Are you ready to dig deep and take a closer look to see what thought patterns are serving you and which ones need to be challenged? What are the things you like about your life creation, so far; the things you value and hold dear? What needs to be built upon and expanded? What patterns need to be released and purged from your life *forever*? What new structures need to be established to create new paradigms that allow you to create life the way you want it.

If you knew today, you had the tools at your disposal to change direction and to create a new reality, would you be ready to learn to use these tools to claim a new life for yourself? If you knew you could not only dream the impossible dream, but actually begin to live that dream; how high would you be willing to reach to get there?

What's Your Story?

In the coaching process, one of the first things I do is to allow my clients to tell their stories. We all have a story. Our story is our own historical explanation of the events in our lives and the people who have been a part of each event. Our stories detail such things as what kind of parents we had and what they did or did not do for us. Did we have siblings, and if so, did we feel they were a positive force in our lives, or did we feel they were a negative force in our upbringing, and why?

Our stories will include things such as friends or the lack of them; our socioeconomic conditions, our talents, drives, accomplishments, and setbacks, and all of the emotional states we have experienced throughout including the ones we are still experiencing. What clearly starts to emerge in the "storytelling" process is the person's interpretation of their life events and situations, and the beliefs and values they have formed from their perception and interpretation. What I discover, without fail, is that the choices they have made, and the resulting actions taken or not taken were always based on those beliefs and values.

When you begin to break down the "life story" in this way, you begin to see how the reality we live in, through our own perception and interpretation of every single experience we encounter has the element of subjectivity. If I am the one interpreting every single thing that happens in my life, and then forming my beliefs and values around my *own* interpretation; it's obvious I must be playing an enormous role in what is showing up for me. "But wait!" You might say. "That is not *really* true." After all you didn't pick your parents or siblings, you didn't have any control over your socioeconomic situation when you were young, and you couldn't help it if you were born with Aunt Mildred's fat gene, right?

But if our lives have been largely determined by the factors that come from our family circumstances, why doesn't everyone's life turn out exactly the same as their siblings, especially ones of the same genders? After all you had the same parents, same siblings, and same religious upbringing; ate the same meals from the same kitchen, and got your body from the same gene pool.

The problem with blaming your life on your parents, your siblings, bad genes, or a bad upbringing is that, oftentimes, one sibling will turn out to be a remarkably successful, well-adjusted, physically fit, and motivated adult; while another one who is close in age and of the same gender becomes a dysfunctional adult… struggling with a lack of achievement and motivation, unsuccessful relationships, and poor self-esteem. Using our upbringing or genetics as our excuse to fail doesn't get us very far, when we realize there are thousands of people whose childhood circumstances and heritage was so much worse than ours; yet, they went on to do amazing things with their lives.

The Stuff Replaying in Your Mind Is What Makes You—You

Since the argument, "I can't be more than the hand of cards I was dealt" doesn't hold up for anyone, what really makes the difference in the outcome in the lives of people, even siblings who basically were brought up in the same life conditions? The conclusion one must make is the difference must lie somewhere inside each of these individuals. To explain the differences in the qualities of life that people experience, we must look to the part of a person that is truly unique—their mind—complete with its own uniquely established thought patterns and filters.

We can think of the mind as our own self-established "government" to all other parts of us. Some of the most powerful examples of the mind's ability to govern our lives and dictate who we become are found in the stories of people, who grew up in seemingly insurmountable life circumstances, but miraculously, through their own mental mastery transcended their circumstances and went on to create lives for themselves that defied the odds.

Dave Pelzer's Story

One of the most personally touching examples is the life story of a man named Dave Pelzer, the author of *A Child Called It*. I met Dave at an author's conference luncheon after hearing him speak to our group in a candid account of his life as a severely physically, mentally, and emotionally abused child. His case had been identified as one of the most disturbing cases of child abuse in California at the time. At age 12, he had been rescued and put into the foster-care system. I carefully listened to Dave describe to an audience of about 600 people, the horrors he had suffered as a child at the hands of his mentally disturbed, alcoholic mother. As I was seated at the table next to him, I then had the unique pleasure of a private hour-long conversation with him, over lunch.

This amazing man is intelligent, optimistic, articulate, handsome, and has a genuinely engaging sense of humor. As we conversed, I was literally in awe of his attitude, his accomplishments, and his depth of character. Because of Dave's resilience, he had overcome a childhood experience that, by his own admission, should have killed him or at the very least caused irreversible psychological damage.

Somehow in spite of the horrific hardships he'd lived through, Dave has gone on to create an extraordinary life for himself. Dave was determined to beat the odds and to better himself in every way possible. When he reached adulthood, he served in the United States Air Force, became a *New York Times* best-selling author, and through his extensive volunteer and service work; he has received numerous commendations and honors from national and global leadership organizations. I am still humbled and inspired by his story and the life he continues to live today. Dave's ability to transcend the worst possible circumstances and to resurrect himself, and his life, is a powerful testament of the magnificence of the human mind and spirit.

Stories like Dave's are good reminders to all of us that the excuses we make for the things that are missing in our lives are just that… excuses.

Harnessing Your Mind's Power

Our mind acts as the interpreter, decision maker, and action taker for the entire person. It is through the vehicle of the mind that we experience joy, peacefulness, creativity, connectedness, grief, sadness, and every other emotional state that is a part of our humanity. It is also through the mind that every thought, belief, and value is formed through our own perception and interpretation. The distinction we must make to reclaim our power over our own lives is one of learning to use our minds, deliberately, not letting our minds use us!

My goal through this program is to help you discover the amazing potential of your mind. This transformational process will set you on a path of learning how destructive or non-productive thought patterns in your mind began, and how to change those self-sabotaging patterns. It will show you how to create new thought patterns that will serve you in your highest aspirations in every area of your life. It will help you program yourself to take action and to make things happen in your life.

Imagine, now, that you can learn how to utilize the brain and its system of thought to change your emotional states from negative states into positive, productive ones. Imagine being able to shift your direction, instantly, to become more productive, motivated, and focused. Most importantly, imagine being able to understand how you can make quantum leaps in your life by changing your focus. By managing your thoughts and thereby managing your reality, you literally begin to create the life of your dreams. This is *your* life. Are you ready to start creating it *now*?

Chapter Two
You Thought You Were Your Thoughts

"Nurture your mind with great thoughts, for you will never go any higher than you think."
—Benjamin Disraeli

Tami came to see me because she had experienced years of chronic health problems. The symptoms included intense pain throughout her body, serious and severe digestive issues, depression, anxiety, and a constant feeling of being overwhelmed. Years of doctors' examinations and extensive testing had gotten her nowhere. No diagnosis, no identifiable disease… inconclusive results. The doctors were baffled and said they could find nothing wrong. Her daily thoughts told her there *was* something wrong with her and she desperately wanted to find out what. I was her last hope.

Our discovery led us to the understanding that she had taken on some of the subconscious programs of her mother, who had always been chronically depressed and not emotionally present for her throughout Tami's childhood. In her mother's world nothing was ever right. Anything that happened usually portended something worse to come. Her fatalistic attitude left Tami with a habitual feeling that she had to be constantly wary of what's around the corner. Even though she had achieved a much higher degree of success and functionality than her mother, she carried her mother's fear consciousness around in her subconscious. It had taught her to anticipate destruction in her body. Tami had learned to navigate life carrying this load of rocks that weighed constantly on her mind and body… living with the feeling that no matter what she achieved or experienced, there was some potentially fatal element underlying it.

Larry came to see me at his mother's insistence. She was so concerned about his despondence and depression that she paid for the appointment. This creative, talented man had almost completely shut down after his girlfriend had broken up with him. In past relationships, he had been the one in control of whether the relationship continued or ended. This event left him with a vicious obsession in which recycling thoughts and images of the woman, who left him, haunted him every minute of his day. His thoughts kept telling him he needed to get back what he had lost because it represented the control he had over his life. Before we started our work together, his mother had considered the possibility that she might need to commit him to a mental institution.

Both Larry and Tami were intelligent, talented people who had experienced significant accomplishment in their careers and had new career opportunities awaiting them. In spite of the success they had achieved in other areas of their life, their errant thought processes were throwing them into states of emotional discord that were debilitating, and creating havoc in all areas of their lives.

Our Most Self-defeating Tendency

The tendency for us to identify with our thoughts is one of the main causes of the dysfunction and turmoil that we experience in our lives. Thinking we are our thoughts is a habit that locks us into a reality we find ourselves yearning to change. Yet, change can never happen, until we develop an understanding of how our mental process "makes" us who we are.

Through my own large family and my clients' shared experiences, I've been privy to a wide variety of people's intimate thoughts and details about their inner lives. I've observed how people manage their thought processes through choice and free will to produce their individual experiences of life. Most people, to a degree, think they are their thoughts. They become their thoughts. They wrap their identity around their thoughts. When all the time, the thoughts and thought patterns that are entrenched in their minds are truly a dynamic moving part that can be changed, modified, and redirected at any moment.

This tendency to think we are our thoughts causes us to believe we are inadequate. It is the habit of thinking we are our thoughts, which causes us to believe we are not loveable or worthy of love. This habit causes us to fear there is something missing within us; a "something" that we imagine would allow us the confidence, success, abundance, and prosperity that we desire so much. This is the habit that chains us to depression and anxiety, and fools us into thinking we are doomed to live with these states forever. Thinking we are our thoughts is the very habit that creates the illusion in our minds that others have more, deserve more, and *are* more than we could ever be. The more firmly our identity is entrenched in our thoughts, the more we feel that our life experience is controlled from somewhere outside ourselves.

Before we can truly move forward to change anything about our life circumstances or situations, we must begin to comprehend the separateness between the thought patterns that continually roll through our brains, and who we truly are. Until we get to the point where we understand that our thoughts are not who we are; we can't create a vision of ourselves doing anything differently in our lives, and we can't imagine being any different than what we've always thought we were.

Thought-identification Traps Us in the Past

Thinking we are our thoughts, or what I call *thought-identification* binds us to our past. All of the thought patterns engrained in our minds, result from the perceptions and emotions that went along with our past experiences. Most of us operate within the thought-identification cycle, until we become aware of it and deliberately take steps to remove ourselves from the cycle. Just as the thousands of thoughts processed from our yesterdays created the reality we live in today, the thoughts we think today will go on to create our futures. It is impossible to be in our greatness when our old thought patterns are telling us we are "not enough" and we believe them, at any level.

What's Going on Behind the Scenes?

In a study published several years ago, the National Science Foundation said that people have as many as 60,000 thoughts per day.[1] It is estimated that around 90 percent of our thoughts are from our days past and only 10 percent are about today. Studies also indicate that anywhere from 75 to 90 percent of those past-based thoughts are negative thoughts that reinforce our fears and perceived inadequacies. In the last ten years there have been thousands of studies done, which have shed a tremendous amount of light on how we process thoughts.

One such study showed that when subjects were asked to solve math equations, the areas of the brain in which we process mathematical calculations clearly showed up on all participants. The interesting thing was that there were five or six other areas of the brain that lit up on each of the subjects, as they were in the middle of their math calculations.[2]

None of the other areas that were lit had anything to do with automatic functions of the body, such as keeping the heart beating or reminding the eyes to blink. The areas that were lit up were other places where the brain processes thoughts. The subjects' conscious minds were still focused on the math problems.

The other observed "thoughts" were being processed below the subjects' conscious awareness. In other words, they were being thought at the subconscious level. What this study demonstrated was the ability of our minds to continue to spontaneously fire thoughts, without us being consciously aware it is happening. Whatever subconscious programs and filters are in place, at any given time, will determine the quality and character of those thoughts being fired. You can be sure that whatever result you are experiencing, at this moment in your life, is predominantly controlled by those deeply entrenched, constantly firing thoughts.

Since the subconscious replays our thoughts like a recorder that always runs, we realize how difficult it would be to shift our lives without deliberate awareness and positive action. Without this awareness we simply wouldn't realize these subconscious thought firings contain programming from our past experiences, and constantly contribute to the essence of who we think we are, and to the quality of our life experience. If we didn't know this subconscious thought activity takes place all of the time inside our heads, we would continue to think life just happens and is beyond our control.

Separation to Challenge the Old and Bring in the New

This recognition of yourself as *separate* from your thoughts doesn't cause specific things to happen in your life. Rather, it allows you to observe your perceptions of the events that happen daily in your life and to modify your beliefs, values, and actions based on a different perception. As you begin to change those beliefs, values, and thereby your actions, specific things *will* begin to happen in your life. Those specific changes and the action you will take to help make them happen—will be in alignment with the new perceptions, beliefs, and values you are now deliberately choosing.

There are people who seem to have it all (solid marriages, nice homes and cars, good jobs, and opportunities to travel and experience new things) and yet, who live with the perception that something is seriously wrong with their lives, and they can't find joy or satisfaction in it. Then there is the kind of person who works two jobs, whose family is packed into small rooms in a small house, but who always has a smile on his face, a word of encouragement for someone else, and a positive outlook on each new day ahead.

Obviously, the difference between these two kinds of people is not their specific circumstances, such as their levels of material comfort or security. The only difference—what makes one feel blessed and fulfilled, and the other one empty and miserable is their perceptions of their lives, as their minds process events through their subconscious thought patterns.

Changing your life circumstances begins with a shift in your awareness. Shifts in awareness not only will open you up to all that is good and positive in your life; it will also help you to change or modify those things about your life you desire to be different.

The separation of your identity from your thoughts is the very thing that allows you to change the channel of your life, to change the story, to modify the theme, to rework the plot and to give you (the main character) an identity based on your greatest, strongest, and most resilient qualities. As you practice separating from conditioned thought processes that previously controlled your choices, they will no longer have a hold on you, and your response to the events in your life, therefore, can be more intentional and deliberate.

The highlight of my work is to be able to play the role of facilitator and witness, as one by one I watch individuals move from a life of suffering to one of freedom. It is fulfilling for me to see people from all walks of life break through to the realization that by understanding and mastering their thought processes, they don't have to accept their lives the way they are. How liberating it is for them to discover it is their own mental filters and programs, which have controlled their perception of the events in their lives... creating beliefs and attitudes that have led to the personal choices that make them who they are.

Can You Really Create Something Different for Yourself?

Coming into an awareness of the personal responsibility that allows each of us to be powerful creators of our own life experience... brings the understanding that we must also have the power to create something different. In other words, if we have been so successful at creating what we don't want, we now can imagine the possibilities of harnessing that creative power and using it deliberately to create what we *do* want. That is why this book has changed the lives of everyone who has read it. We all have things we want to change about our lives and ourselves. It is a universal human condition. Most people just don't know where to start.

For people to go from complete immersion in one understanding of reality, to developing a new understanding of reality usually requires real effort and commitment on their part. The habits of depression, anxiety, and lack of confidence; inability to take action, unsuccessful relationships, or lack of success in finance and/or a career don't die easily. Those habits have usually been repeated and perfected within a person's thought processes so many times over the years, that the habit has become an entrenched pattern carried out systematically by the subconscious mind.

You may be wondering why I would refer to states such as depression and anxiety as habits. You might argue that they are illnesses. Although modern medicine has categorized these as illnesses, *in most cases,* states of depression, anxiety, and even suicidal thinking exist because the person experiencing them has interpreted events, formed beliefs and values *around* his or her life events, and assigned specific rules to those beliefs and values. These rules make it *impossible* for the person to succeed at the things he or she values the most in life.

When success in the areas of life that people most highly value seems impossible, they are left with the feelings of uncontrollable fear (anxiety), feelings of complete overwhelm (depression), and feelings of absolute desperation (suicide). That is not to invalidate experiences of intense states of dysfunction, such as clinical depression. People *really* do feel these states intensely. They suffer intensely. But unless they're dealing with acute, situational depression or anxiety brought on by a sudden unexpected event, the reality is these states are usually manifested through a lifetime of mental processing.

In the study of NLP, we learn that the brain must distort, delete, or generalize *all* of the information it takes in or we would literally go crazy with sensory overload. There are about two million bits of information per minute coming at us through various sensory stimuli. Our brains can process approximately seven of the two million. We filter this information through language, memories, attitudes, values, beliefs, decisions, and time and space. Our own internal representation is then made based on those micro-choices that our mental filters have processed. This internal representation which includes feelings, pictures, and sounds puts us in a state of mind, which in turn produces our behaviors and physiology changes. This *all* happens in a fraction of a second and can be part of a feedback loop, where our physiology can work in reverse motion to change our attitudes, and our behavior can affect our language.

The drawing below represents the cycle that is constantly taking place between us and our world.

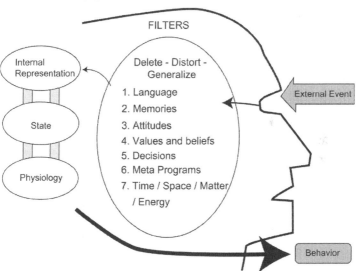

Part of our life experience includes enduring challenging situations and events. All of us, at some point in our lives have probably experienced a state of mind that felt overwhelming and debilitating. These states keep us from being productive, successful and happy. When we go through challenging times like this, we often wonder how we could get to such a low place. We wonder how this state of suffering we would never *want* to experience, began. That question can be answered by examining the way we process the events in our world through our mind. These low states begin with a thought or a pattern of thought. Instead of processing feelings, such as depression or sadness as an experience, our mind begins to allow thoughts that confuse the experience with our *very identity*.

When people step into my office for the first time, often, they are in complete solidarity with their own suffering. When they experience the habits of depression, anxiety, desperation, or hopelessness for long periods of time, those states can eventually become a big part of their identities. They feel depressed, so their thoughts begin to tell them this is who they are. As in all initial sessions we begin with the story-telling process. In this storytelling process they will say things like "I am depressed," "I am anxiety ridden," "I am suicidal," and "I am unhappy." An "I am" statement is a strong statement of identity. What they are really saying is, "this state that I am experiencing is who I am." When you rephrase it this way, it seems a little ridiculous doesn't it?

This Temporary State of Mind Is Not Who You Are?

It might sound ridiculous, but people experiencing suffering *truly* believe that their suffering *is* a part of their identity, or in extreme cases, all of their identity. They believe they *are* a depressed person and are doomed to this state forever. They believe they *are* an anxious person who may lose control at any moment. They may even believe they are hopeless and always will be, and have nothing to live for.

In cases where the state of suffering has gone on for many years, it has taken over their lives and completely defined who they are. The acceptance of a particular negative state as their identity has also radiated out to all areas of their life. If they have lived any of these identities of dysfunction for any length of time, the members of their family have also had to live it with them, especially in their closest relationships, as with a spouse or children. In such situations, the state of dysfunction has also gone on to dictate and define the other important areas of their lives, such as their willingness to do new things or accept new challenges, being present and available to the people who love them, or allowing their creativity to flow in their lives.

Middle class and affluent people sometimes make the mistake of thinking that negative states of being, and the dysfunction they can cause within families are limited to people on the lower levels of the socioeconomic ladder; as if only people who live in trailer homes and shop at Wal-Mart have the kind of problems that traumatize the members of their families on an ongoing basis. Nothing could be further from the truth. The clients I see range from being multi-millionaire surgeons to people who have been out of work much of their adult lives.

The dilemma of how to manage the constant thought-emotion feedback loop that has so much control over our lives does not discriminate by income or by education level. It simply exists as part of the human condition. Learning to understand it and master it is what defines the level of happiness, success, and contentment we will experience within our lifetime.

Karen's Story

Karen made an appointment with me after hearing me speak on a radio talk show about the power of hypnotherapy in releasing old thought patterns and energy, and creating a new reality for ourselves. When we met for the first time, she was firmly entrenched in her identity as a depressed person.

Karen had horrible memories from childhood. One such memory was of her mother swinging her around by the ankle, as a toddler, and releasing her to slam into the refrigerator. Another memory was of the day her mother left for good. Afterwards, her father did his best to care for his three young daughters on his own. But several months later, like his wife, he also threw in the towel. He loaded his two year old, four year old, and eight year old daughters into his truck and drove them to the homes of various relatives, where the adults all argued about who should keep the children.

A very painful recollection that stuck out in Karen's mind was hearing the adults discuss the importance of taking care of the baby and the four-year-old, but suggesting that eight-year-old Karen wasn't as much of a concern because she was older and could take care of herself. She vividly remembered chasing after her father's truck crying and begging him not to go, as he drove away for good. Until Karen reached age 18, she kept being passed around from family to family. She basically played a Cinderella role in the homes of her relatives; each family using her for her ability to work until they couldn't afford to feed her anymore. Then they moved her on the next family.

The rejection Karen experienced, and the worthlessness she felt about herself were overwhelming to her. Even though she had a good work ethic and had always held a job, she had lived with depression all of her life. Her depressive state had greatly impacted her relationships and it defined her sense of self. One of the things she shared in telling me her "story" was that she had cried every single day of her life. She was 62 years old at the time. It was clear to me that Karen's self-defeating thoughts, from a lifetime of rejection, had become her identity.

The beliefs Karen had formed about herself from her interpretation of her life's events went something like this:

- "I am not worthy of anyone's time and attention."
- "I don't deserve attention and affection."
- "There isn't anything lovable about me."
- "I don't deserve love."
- "Why would someone want me in their life?"
- "I am not worthy of love."
- "I just want to die. There is no reason to live."

The identity she had developed had given her a life with little joy. Her self-defeating thoughts became Karen's firm beliefs about her identity. Deeply embedded thought patterns of being unlovable, unwanted, and unworthy became who she was. She had frequently experienced the feeling that she would have been better off dead.

We had our work cut out for us. I started by using EFT to clear the fears and rejection that Karen carried in her nervous system. Using this technique, I led her back through the events that triggered her excruciating emotional pain, to fully experience it again. Within that context, we began to reframe the thoughts that had supported her self-defeating beliefs. While tapping through the meridian points on Karen's body, we changed beliefs like, "My mom left me because I wasn't lovable" to the new belief that went something like this: "My poor mother's mental illness made it impossible for her to cope with the responsibilities of motherhood. How sad that must have been for her. I'm thankful I don't suffer the way she did."

Other beliefs, such as "Nobody ever wanted me; I was older and unlovable," were reframed as "Everybody in my extended family did the best they could. These problems took place during the Great Depression in the 1930's, and money was so scarce for all of my aunts and uncles. They saw that I was older and therefore more capable than my younger sisters. I have always been competent and capable. People can count on me."

During each session, Karen and I would use clearing, going back into each emotionally painful memory she still had. After the tapping session, I would induce a light trance-state of hypnotherapy to access her deeper subconscious mind… to accept new beliefs and reframe the painful memories into more positive or even neutral ones. We also used a technique that took her back to each stage of her childhood, healing her inner child-self at each stage, and going through a forgiveness process to release anger and blame toward family members who had played a role in her suffering at those stages.

By utilizing coaching techniques in the fully conscious state, EFT for releasing fears that were locked into the nervous system, and hypnotherapy to access the power of her subconscious mind, Karen began to have massive breakthroughs. Thankfully and miraculously in only five sessions, Karen felt completely free of the crushing depression she had experienced for most of her life! She started to reorganize her home and her life. She set new goals to get out socially and was ready for some new relationships in her life. She sent me a beautiful and heartwarming e-mail expressing her gratitude that I had come into her life, and helped her free herself of the crushing, debilitating depression that had controlled each day of her life, and had dominated her identity up to that point.

I feel truly grateful to be able to help facilitate important transformations such as Karen's, in the lives of my clients. It is so inspiring for me to see them begin to live a much better life than the one that was making them so miserable before. I am continually amazed this phenomenal transformation all takes place in the mind/body through the power of thought. For a free manual on EFT go to: **www.crystaldwyer.com/eft.html**

Growth and Change Mean Something Different to Everyone

Not everyone's life experience has been as painful or extreme as Karen's. What I've learned through my work, however, is that even people who are functioning very well in some areas of their lives usually have other areas in which they feel a deep sense of emptiness or lack of fulfillment. All of us have room in our lives to accommodate growth. Growth and change can mean something different to everyone.

If you never finished college and you feel it's too late for you, change may include getting rid of your limiting beliefs about college education only being for a specific age group, and following up with a plan of action. If you've had a phenomenal career but have never had the meaningful, lasting relationship you've always desired, change for you could mean deliberately observing your beliefs about having love, deserving love, and giving love. Doing so may cause you to redefine your values in those areas, and the rules you've attached to those values that may be sabotaging your long-term success in relationships.

Growth and change can also mean a complete change of identity for some. When you really begin the excavation process into the subconscious mind, and step back from your programmed thoughts to observe them; you may find that the thing you always *thought* you were supposed to do or be was actually someone else's idea of what you are supposed to do or be.

This powerful epiphany can cause a high-paid business executive to quit the corporate world and open a floral shop. It can motivate a 20-year stay-at-home mom to go back and get a law degree. It can convert high-paid accountants into full-time stay-at-home mothers. The process can cause an undervalued, unappreciated wife who has given up her identity for her husband's success and career to strike out on her own and end the marriage. It can even inspire someone, who has already made their millions in the corporate or entertainment world, to spend time in poverty-stricken countries and spearhead organizations that make important differences in our world. I have had clients who have done all of these things.

Processing Life's Traumas and Moving Forward

As sad as it is to witness the pain that some people have had to experience, such as in Karen's case, I know that as a facilitator for permanent change and healing, I must help people to *release* the old emotional and mental patterns that have kept them trapped in their pain. The only way I can truly help them is to help them empower themselves to move past the painful experience.

When someone we love has experienced a traumatic event, our natural human compassion compels us to relate to their pain and provide validation for the things they are feeling and experiencing. The validation process plays an important role in permanently healing past issues. However, what often happens within supportive relationships is that the supporter helps keep the experience alive past the point that it serves the victim. If we participate in reliving the pain over and over again with the victim (and sometimes this will go on for years) the victim-mentality gets reinforced and is perpetuated until it becomes—like any other repetitive thought pattern—the very identity of the person we love. When we do this, we are providing reasons for our loved ones to continue to stay in the emotional and mental space of victimhood.

After an initial stage of empathy and validation, our role as supporters should be to help our loved ones find healthy, positive ways to feel significance and importance other than the story of being hurt or wounded. Staying in a victim identity will ultimately destroy the person, not serve him or her.

The healing process I take my clients through, using EFT, allows them to be fully in their emotional pain and release it. EFT has the effect of helping to discharge much of the emotional pain people feel and carry throughout their entire bodies. Then by inducing a light trance state through hypnotherapy, we work through the process of neutralizing the emotions and reframing the thought patterns that supported the negative emotions, and we begin introducing a new perspective about the person or people who played the perpetrator's role in that particular traumatic event. After this, it is very important to go through a forgiveness process.

Whether or not traumatized people ever actually forgive their perpetrators in person… going through the subconscious exercise of doing so allows them to experience it in their own reality. In this way, they can truly detach from the person who caused them pain, and move into a new reality, where they begin to create a new life for themselves.

Both the Problem and the Solution Exist in the Mind

You may be wondering how these techniques could be effective if the process is happening only in the mind. The conscious mind is the only part of the mind's awareness that is able to discern truth from non-truth. The subconscious mind has no truth discernment mechanism. It simply stores patterns.

Think about it. Most negative thought patterns that run at the subconscious level don't contain a shred of truth; yet, we believe them and operate by them as if they are true. If your subconscious mind carries a thought message that says, "You can't be a successful salesperson; you don't have what it takes." Is that true? If you have a mouth, eyes, ears, arms, legs, and a brain then of course it is not true. In fact, you could be missing any one of those bodily characteristics, except for the brain, and *still* be a successful salesperson! But if self-defeating thoughts cycle through your subconscious mind enough times, you will develop a subconscious belief about not having what it takes to be a successful salesperson and your choices and actions will follow your beliefs; thus preventing you from becoming the success you know in your heart you could be.

Your beliefs about yourself generated through your thoughts, via your brain are really the *only* thing that will create or prevent your success in any area of life—period. Remember, our thoughts aren't necessarily real or unreal. They are simply the internal representations our minds make as we process the world around us.

Looking back into my own life I realize I became interested, at a very young age, in how people could perceive and interpret a given situation so differently. I was the third child in a family of nine children: six girls and three boys. The social order that emerged in our large family; everyone's role and perspective in it both fascinated and baffled me. We were all being raised with the same values and expectations that came from the same mother and father; yet, we would form different conclusions about situations that arose. We each felt varying levels of responsibility. We each had different expectations of ourselves, each other, and of our parents. Some of us couldn't wait to leave our small town as soon as we got the chance and get on to something bigger. Others couldn't imagine leaving everything they had always known. They are still there.

Even with our shared upbringing and gene pool, our individual thought processes served to shape nine different human beings with diverse beliefs, values, and rules, which to this day shape our individuality and approach to life. Each of our own minds made different internal representations of the outside stimuli that were so similar.

Human beings are funny creatures. There are some folks who just refuse to believe that what their thoughts tell them or what their life circumstances are… is not necessarily who they are. They literally feel attached to their conditions and environment no matter how miserable it is because of the certainty it provides them. They know what to expect and they refuse to imagine things being any different. It doesn't make any sense, logically, that we would be attached to the very thought and behavior patterns that make us miserable. Our tendency to think we *are* those thoughts, and the part of our brain that finds safety in the predictability of habits (even bad ones) are the two things that keep us trapped in the sameness of life through our old thought patterns.

Life Change Starts with Awareness and Desire

When we develop the awareness and desire to make life changes by redirecting and modifying our thoughts to effectively change our thought patterns, we can literally create new lives for ourselves. Essentially, everyone has the power within, through the vehicle of the mind, to recognize the entrenchment of thought patterns that are not serving them, to identify their attachment to those patterns, and to activate their own free will and ability to change them.

If we are willing to challenge the status quo and see ourselves as separate from old thoughts and what they've created, then comes the fun part. We suddenly find that we *can* learn to consciously and deliberately create new thoughts. As our beliefs shift and our choices shift with them, we discover all kinds of new opportunities for ourselves. It is an exhilarating discovery process when you begin to learn to separate your identity from your thoughts, and then to test the creative power of each of your thoughts. Eventually this process will lead you to getting in touch with your deepest dreams. It involves giving yourself permission to say:

- "I can have what I want in this life."
- "I can achieve any level of success I desire."

- "I don't have to be a victim of this pain."

- "I am not going to be a victim of this suffering, worry, and anxiety."

- "I will no longer be a victim of depression."

- "I refuse to be overwhelmed and indecisive anymore."

- "I can achieve excellence in any area."

You do not have to accept the thoughts and emotional patterns that have caused you to live with any conditions that don't serve your highest good or greatest possible achievement in life. All of these things and more can change. All of these things were directed by your own thoughts, many at the subconscious level. As you progress through the remaining chapters, you will develop a new awareness and learn to master the tools that will help you create a life with your *own* signature on it.

You Are Not Your Thoughts

The brain processes all of your identity, successes, accomplishments, values, and beliefs through thoughts. Your thoughts are the vehicle; the *modus operandi,* so to speak that creates any state you will ever experience. Learning how thoughts work and how to direct them in a positive way will give you the power to make the choices that will create the life you might have previously thought was impossible.

Chapter Three
Anatomy of a Thought

"Be a master of mind rather than mastered by mind."
—*Zen proverb*

Now that we've had some discussion about thoughts and the power they have to create our experience of life; it might be a good time to ask the question: What is a thought? What actually occurs in the brain at the physiological level when the phenomenon we call "thought" happens? This chapter discusses the events that take place in the brain when a thought occurs. The brain is involved in everything we do. It is the clearinghouse for our lives. The more we understand what occurs in our psycho-neurological system to shape who we are, the more empowered we become. Knowledge is power.

Your Brain: The Ultimate Computer

How often do you stop to think about this amazing organ we call the brain? The brain is a truly miraculous structure… allowing us as human beings autonomy and dominion over the entire living Earth. Experts say that the human brain is much more highly complex than the entire World Wide Web, many times over. The cell connections in your brain outnumber the stars in the universe. If you had an advanced piece of technical equipment and you wanted to learn to use that piece of equipment to your greatest advantage, you would probably take the time to learn how that equipment functions. Think of your brain as a highly refined, highly complex, yet fragile computer. If you learn as much as you can about this fascinating operating system inside your skull, it will help you move toward the mastery you desire over your life.

The human brain has a predetermined structure that is universal within our species. The brain has evolved to the point it is at today, largely due to the behavior and experiences of our ancient ancestors. Their behavior and experiences caused the brain to form new neural connections to adapt to the environment around them. Many of those traits and abilities that were necessary for survival became encoded into the human brain cells as part of our brain patterning; literally making those traits and abilities part of our DNA. The very structure of the human brain changed through choices that were made and behaviors that were modified—in order to survive the conditions and respond to the stimuli that human beings faced in the world at that time. The brain that we *Homo sapiens* are endowed with today is a product of that evolutionary process. One of the long-term genetic qualities that we universally inherited is that we process various kinds of sensory information in the same general regions of the brain.

In addition to this heritage, another genetic contribution comes into play in the data processing center called the brain. This is a shorter-term genetic contribution, which comes from our parents, grandparents, and great-grandparents. Some of the personality traits we carry come from the patterns of nerve connections that wired the brains of those that came before us. We actually can inherit patterns that contribute to things, such as our mannerisms, facial expressions, intellect and coordination and even our tendencies in emotional matters. If you notice little traits about yourself like you bark when you laugh, or you tend to get mushier than most people do when watching sad or romantic movies, chances are you would find someone before you in your genetic line; perhaps your mother, your aunt, or even your great-grandma who carries this same tendency.

The family members who came before us interacted with the environment they were in, and then the information that was processed and laid down in the neural circuitry of their brains shaped and molded their DNA. As couples come together and create new families the combinations of the DNA of their brains are present in their offspring. We come into this world with both a long-term and short-term genetic inheritance of the experiences of those who have gone before us. These genetic qualities give us the basic structure and function of our brains, as well as some of our individual qualities.

Is Your Destiny Preordained by Your Genes? Science Says No

Does genetic inheritance mean that the way we will think, feel, react, and behave is fixed and unchangeable? Absolutely not. In fact, when we examine the way our ancestors influenced changes in their own brain patterning, we see how *our* environment and *our* reaction to it could also powerfully influence and change the structure of our own brains, down to the very DNA of our individual brain and nerve cells. This is a permanent, ongoing quality of the living cells in our bodies, and especially in our brains. As with our ancient ancestors and our recent forbearers *our* behaviors, reactions, and choices continue to change, remold, and reshape the very wiring of our operating vehicle—our brain. This is the way our thoughts become our anatomy.

In his groundbreaking book, *The Biology of Belief* (Mountain of Love, 2005), cell biologist and researcher, Bruce Lipton, Ph.D. discusses the newest discoveries in the science of *epigenetics*. In Latin, "epigenetics" means "control above genetics." Dr. Lipton says that the last decade of research has established that genes themselves don't provide the control for our lives. He contends that environmental influences (like stress, nutrition, pollution, and emotions) can modify our DNA without changing its basic blueprint. This remarkable research demonstrates that the physiology and behavior of cells are determined when an environmental signal "unsleeves" the protein sleeve that allows a gene to be "read." The gene cannot be read without a signal outside the gene to remove the protein covering. Depending on what the environmental signal is, there can actually be 2000 variations that happen from a given gene blueprint. The outside signals, in fact, modify the gene! Those modifications to genes can actually be passed down to future generations.[1]

Think of what this means in regard to our genetic potential, for anything from musical genius to diseases with a known genetic component. What environment would it take to foster genius? What environmental conditions allow for disease to come through?

Our own environmental experiences become hard-wired into the brain and other parts of our body, just as our genetic wiring is. Our learning and memories lay down neural circuitry and chemistry to become our biology. This circuitry begins to shape who we are as a person and how we relate to our world. *Neuroplasticity* is a term frequently used by researchers, today, in discussions about this remarkable ability of the brain to learn new information from outside stimuli and experience, and to encode into memory the learning that takes place from those experiences of life.

What does this mean for mastering your thought processes and improving your life? The flexibility of our functioning brain, which allows us to rework the wiring laid down by previous experience and to create new connections through learning, also enables us to master our states of mind and develop new understandings. In this way, we humans can continue to evolve even within this very lifetime.

Remodeling My Brain

Neuroplasticity is the functional quality of the brain that essentially *allows us to recreate ourselves.* I'll try to explain the concept of neuroplasticity in the simplest way possible.

The brain contains somewhere around 100 billion *neurons,* or nerve cells. In fact, the greatest numbers of nerve cells that are found in the body are found in the brain. These nerve cells are linked together in *neural networks,* which start forming as soon as we begin learning—when we're domiciled in the womb awaiting our entry into the world. Something as simple as feeling our mothers breathe more deeply as they begin to relax… links information into a nice little neural network that is stored inside our developing head, which by the way, is bigger and heavier than the rest of our body combined when we're at that stage. Tiny nerve cells join together in different arrangements and combinations every time something new or different happens. As those moments of learning or happenings are repeated, the neural connections are strengthened and become learned memories. They become patterns which we eventually rely upon, to process other stimuli and events that come in from outside of us, for the rest of our lives.

Millions of neural groupings or *neural networks* are consistently being formed throughout our childhood, since so many experiences are new to us during our formative years. These connections literally make anatomical changes in our brains, and those changes cause changes in our bodies, our beliefs, and our attitudes. Thus, they become changes in our lives.

My Adult Brain Can Still Change and Grow?

As we get older, we still have the ability to *continue* to change. The plasticity of the brain doesn't stop when we reach adulthood. As adults, many of us stop expecting change in our lives and begin to settle for what i*s*—simply because we aren't aware of this innate quality our brains have to allow us to change what is. Neuroplasticity is the ability within our brains to let go of an old habitual pattern and fire a new pattern, which creates new conditions in our lives. By focusing on new thoughts and imagining new scenarios, we cause bunches of nerve cells to join together by chemical messages and change the anatomy of our brains every time we do it. There is nothing fixed about our brains. We can make our brains change and grow, just by deliberately directing our thoughts.

New Beginnings for Everyone

Breakthroughs in brain science demonstrate that we no longer need to hold the belief that we are doomed to the destiny of an inferior gene combination, or that our level of success or achievement is limited to that of our family. Most importantly, research shows us we don't have to be enslaved to the belief patterns we have integrated into ourselves, which might have helped create a personal identity we don't want as our own. Just knowing that our brains come equipped with the capability to change destructive or non-productive beliefs and attitudes can become a life-altering event. Many of the belief patterns that we operate from, on a daily basis, cause us a tremendous amount of turmoil and dysfunction. Understanding the reality of the remarkable malleability of the brain's operating system makes us aware that we have a choice to stop repeating those belief patterns, which have not served our highest potential and to choose ones that will.

The nerve cells in our brains communicate with each other using little arm-like structures that look like the branches and roots of a tree. When they pass electrochemical information along to each other they don't actually touch. The neurochemical information actually "jumps" a gap between the ends of the nerve. This gap is called a *synapse*. When a thought occurs, an electrically charged ion shoots through a neuron like a bolt of lightning. But there is never just one nerve cell firing at a time in your brain. A single thought or action creates a thunderstorm of activity. Literally, millions of nerve cells fire in the brain during any activity including sleep. The thoughts, behaviors, and habits we have *now* are there because they have been fired again and again in our brains creating a firmly entrenched pattern, which helps to create the reality we exist in each day.

When a new thought or concept is introduced to the brain, it is weak; so it attaches to a stronger neuron connecting to other neurons and forging a new sequence and direction, like little rivulets that suddenly have fresh water flowing in a new direction. To change our lives and make something new or different happen, we must make something new happen in our brain. We must either learn something new, open up to a new understanding, or have a new experience. Every time we do we make a new synaptic connection.

If we are complacent in allowing the same predictable thoughts, habits, and behaviors to repeat, again and again, not much will change in our reality or life experience. The repetition of those thought patterns will keep producing the reality we are already getting in life.

How Do I Start to Make the Change?

There are two things you have to do to set this in motion. First, you must stop firing the same old thoughts that reinforce the strength of the old synaptic connections. Second, you must deliberately choose new thoughts, which create different neurochemical connections and pathways. Think of the new neural pathways being forged as if you were discovering a new direction to go in an overgrown jungle. The first time you push your way through slicing through the foliage, it takes more effort and even seems difficult. The more times you decide to go down that same path, however, the easier it becomes. You have broken it in. It becomes a well-worn thought path that is a breeze to traverse when you repeatedly direct a thought that way. The more you repeat those thoughts, the more they become the improved and evolved pathways of thinking. Those new pathways will offer you different perceptions, beliefs, values, and actions and eventually different outcomes in your life.

Repetition is the key to creating new thought pathways and allowing ones that are no longer useful to become overgrown, unused, and weak. Repetition of new ideas, thoughts, and concepts causes a deeper bonding between neurons in the brain. When we think something or act something out over and over again, it creates a well-connected, well-developed neurochemical pattern in the brain. In this way, we eventually are able to cause thoughts and behaviors to happen automatically. Attitudes, behaviors, and activities that at one time might have seemed foreign to us begin to occur, as if we have always been thinking them or doing them.

This reality applies to things we think and do that we dislike about our lives and ourselves, *and* things we would love to integrate into our lives and ourselves, so that they would become natural and automatic. The working operation of our brain does not filter or discriminate. What you focus on and repeat, again and again, will eventually create entrenched thought patterns that fire automatically; thus, creating your beliefs, attitudes, and your course of action (or lack of it) in virtually *every* aspect of your life.

Stop Preparing for the Worst!

There is a common tendency in human behavior to put our greatest focus on the things we don't like, the things we want to avoid, the things that cause us pain, and the things we fear the most coming to pass. Many of us have integrated the belief that if we keep those negatives on our radar screens all of the time, somehow, we will be more prepared for them; we'll be able to either to manage them better or to avoid them. Ironically, the opposite is true. The brain wiring is such that those things we put our attention *on*, fire as thoughts in our brain making connections with other neural patterns. By focusing on potentially negative outcomes or problems that could arise, we essentially keep creating and reinforcing the thought patterns that will lead to the beliefs and actions that will eventually bring about *what we are focusing on*. Instead of helping us better manage or avoid problems… focusing on them and worrying or obsessing about them actually will create more problems in our lives; the very ones we thought we could avoid by worrying about them all the time.

Creating Your Own Masterpiece

When we come into this lifetime the brain is equipped with a neurological foundation, which is our long-term and short-term genetic inheritance. It is then through our experience and the choices we make throughout our experiential journey that personalize and individualize the person we become.

If you think of *you* as a beautifully intricate painting your genetic inheritance would be the first broad brushstrokes. The detail, color, and texture that complete the entire masterpiece, which becomes the *self*, are being added all the time through your experience and more importantly through the perceptions, beliefs, and attitudes you *choose* as you experience this journey called life.

It is an important beginning to understand the working brain's role in our reality as a human being. The brain is the vehicle we have to express our souls. To achieve mastery over our lives, we must first understand this evolutionary miracle that is our brain. This highly complex processing center is ours to utilize as we progress and evolve in this lifetime. It is crucial to understand the role and function of the brain to achieve balance, success, and happiness in life. However, as fascinating and miraculous as our brain is, the real power directing our lives is not found in the brain.

As we move forward, through the remaining chapters in this book, we will go beyond the discussion of the brain itself and focus on the director of the brain: the choice maker—the real *you*.

Chapter Four

History Lesson: Studying Your Family's Belief/Behavior Patterns

*"Other things may change us. But we start
and end with the family"*
—*Anthony Brandt*

⚜

When you make the decision to really under stand your life and to deliberately make the most of it, looking back down the road you've walked, so far, is an important component of the transformation process. The most obvious place to start is your experience of childhood and adolescence in your own family. Your family life was the training ground and your initiation into how people act, think, perceive, and believe. Since your mind was so malleable at a young age (a mind full of mush as they say), you most certainly integrated the impressions and perceptions of your siblings and parents into your own experience. Ultimately, your own impressions and perceptions (influenced by those around you all of the time) became your beliefs and values and started directing your actions and your sense of identity.

Your Childhood Story

I always start out by doing an in-depth intake of personal information when a new client comes to see me: the storytelling process. Invariably, childhood and adolescent experiences will be part of the discussion. So impressionable is the mind of a young child, that neural connections are being formed at breakneck speed and quantities in the early years. During these young years, our beliefs, values, intelligence, and even our emotional tendencies are being dramatically sculpted through our family interactions and experiences. There really is no way we can emerge unenlightened or unscathed (whichever the case may be) from our daily interactions and experiences with the group we call our family. Our families provide the feedback, social interaction, and social structure that we need to develop our skills to survive in the world. More importantly, our family experience provides the emotional foundation that we will move forward with into our adult years.

Some of us reach adulthood with a rather shaky emotional foundation that can be rocked, even when the light winds of life's basic challenges blow through. Other fortunate ones have had such an emotionally stable and consistent home life (through childhood) that they can ride out a life's-coming-atcha hurricane, fairly unscathed.

So many neural networks were formed during the years of our youth, that to achieve optimal success or transformation in our lives, we must examine the thought patterns that were downloaded into our young brains and discern if they are serving us in the adult world. To know how we were affected and how our sense of "self" was influenced; we must take an honest look at the issues and any dysfunctional themes that were prevalent in our family landscape. Since parents are the ones we rely on the most for our psychological and emotional stability, their psychological and emotional states most definitely have influenced how our mental and emotional programming is put together.

Which Family Members Still Live in Your Mind?

There are probably many ways our parents were able to provide positive support and nurturing to us. This helped create the mental software for us to develop some of the most positive characteristics we carry today. There are also many ways that negative neural patterns could have been set. Those negative program pieces can often keep undoing a lot of the things we are trying to get done. Undiscovered childhood programming can keep coming back to sabotage our forward progression in life, until we identify it and take steps to disconnect from the negativity and change the programming. This allows us to purge the dysfunctional patterns, so that we don't keep passing them down to future generations.

If either of your parents was plagued with depression, it may have left you with programming that says it is your job to make everything right. Children who live with a constant concern that the very people they are supposed to rely upon for strength and support are *not* reliable—take on an adult caretaking role—long before they have the psychological readiness. Adults who had this childhood experience often carry a belief system that says it is up to them to make sure that everyone else is happy and okay. This belief system creates an underlying sense of hopelessness, since it is an impossible task to make everyone else in your life happy. Carrying this belief structure throughout your life can cause you to feel constantly overwhelmed and disempowered.

If you had a parent who was unpredictably volatile, angry, or violent, you could have ended up with a belief system that keeps telling you your world could fall apart at any minute. It tells you that you can never know when everything that seems stable and fine could blow up, and that life really is not safe or secure. Living with beliefs like this can cause chronic anxiety and even debilitating panic attacks. Your belief system controls your life and prevents you from moving forward and taking the risks that are necessary to succeed.

If there was a history of sexual abuse, not just by a parent but by any family member, you could be living with a deep sense of powerlessness and fear. The fear usually comes from the threats that are made by the perpetrator to keep the abuse secret. Feelings of guilt and shame can go on into adulthood because children will blame themselves. A child may feel he or she is a "bad" person because he or she "let" this happen.

If a man has a father who never approves of him he grows up with deep anger and resentment. The fear that his dad was right can create a belief system that causes him to fail at everything he tries. He believes at a deep level that he is never good enough. He is not consciously aware that he carries these beliefs; yet, he experiences a tremendous amount of frustration and low self-esteem from his inability to create a successful career for himself. The belief system keeps recreating a cycle of negativity, lack of ambition, and a self-sabotaging follow-through pattern whenever he starts something worthwhile, such as a new job or career.

These are just some of the basic patterns that I have seen with clients. There are many more. Each of these patterns had their beginnings in familial interactions and relationships.

Can This Map Get You to Where You Want to Go?

Our immersion in our family dynamics, and all of the emotional and mental patterning that directed those dynamics… was responsible for creating the first versions of our mental and emotional maps. Whether we want to admit it or not, we have characteristics and personality traits that are a direct result of our family members' presence in our lives, during our early years. It's ironic, but some of the qualities and characteristics that are a part of our own structure are the very ones we can't tolerate in other members of our families. It is very difficult for us to identify such things within ourselves, without dissecting the emotional and mental patterns contained in our family histories.

The family circle or intimate partnerships seem to be the stage where our biggest emotional dramas are acted out. This is why it is important in the life transformation process to carefully observe ourselves in these familial settings. Noticing what triggers our emotional states, and how we respond when different states are triggered is a great starting point in uncovering our own mental and emotional map.

Once we have taken a clear and honest look at the way we've mapped our perceptions, beliefs, and thought patterns; then we can decide if this personal map we've been following will ever actually get us where we *want* to go. It is within the roles of being siblings, spouses, parents, and children that we get our proverbial "buttons" pushed more than any other place. It is also within the context of these familial interactions that we unleash our truest most unedited responses. We generally feel safer to do so around those who know us best; whose lives are connected to ours by ties that are more durable and intimate than friendship or casual acquaintance.

Cutting Destructive Family Cords

As the family was the initial staging area in the formation of our perceptions, beliefs, and experiences, the emotional states we take forward into our lives often become associated in our minds, with the people we call family. Since our primary interactions were with family members during those formative years, they are also usually the ones to whom we have developed neural patterns of attachment. Well-established thought patterns run subconsciously, and they can be either negative or positive depending on what was happening during those early years when the thought pattern was formed.

Even as adults, many of us can relate to feelings that have triggered the thought, "I want my mommy (or daddy as the case may be)." In a moment of weakness or defeat, how many capable, functioning adults think of calling a parent for comfort? I would say the number is pretty high. In such cases, we have attached the experience of needing and getting comfort to a parent.

Of course, many adults had childhood relationships with their parents that were complicated or marred by strife and turmoil. Many of those adults experienced enough confusion or negativity in youth that they have attached that negativity to a parent. The thought patterns they carry from their youth have resulted in a fixed belief that their parents can't be relied upon. These adults often have a developed program of abandonment and a lack of emotional trust, in any of their relationships.

Family-based neural attachment patterns can become pretty complicated and quite rigid by adulthood, because of the unfiltered rawness of the emotions we feel as children and adolescents. Intense emotion, whether it is exuberantly happy, desperately sad, or riddled with deep anger causes stronger neurochemical thought patterns to form in the brain. What is encoded into our brains during our upbringing is firmly rooted, whether we know it or not.

The most common neural attachments to our family members are usually subtle and have a sort of insidious quality about them. I've seen many women who have always felt the need to please their father and win his love and affection. These women are driven, successful, and accomplished individuals. They seem to be functioning very well in their lives, but underneath the success and achievement is the constant worry that they are never quite enough. They keep *doing more* to keep up with the demands of a psychological program they aren't even aware of. When we delve into the family history and review the dynamic and the interaction that existed at the time the women were forming their psychological foundation, the source of this demanding, self-defeating program becomes apparent.

The important thing is to not go into blame and resentment, when we discover who is at the other end of our family neural attachments. Most of the fathers in these cases truly wanted the best for their daughters. They never wanted their daughter to be left out in the cold by an uncaring man. The best solution they could see was to teach their daughters an unrelenting standard of perfection that they thought would never fail them.

The Family Blame Game

There are people who have experienced intense difficulty in their youth, and have carried these negative emotional and thought attachments to certain family members for most of their lives. They end up developing a perception that *everything* that is wrong with their lives is because of something a sibling or parent did or didn't do for them. There *are* extreme cases where there was physical, sexual, or mental abuse, and the experience was so harsh and severe that it is difficult for adults to disengage the life experience they face today, from the person who abused or neglected them during their years of innocence. These cases require intervention from a therapist, who is trained to support and guide survivors of abuse through a releasing and detaching process, so they can begin to live independently of their abuser's residue.

In most cases, however, negative attachments actually start to form as a result of normal human interaction between family members. Something in the familial interaction (which was accompanied by intense emotions) caused distorted perceptions, which lead to distorted negative thinking, which lead to distorted beliefs. People then operate with the belief that this sibling, parent, or other family member, somehow is the key to their misery and should be blamed for any problem that plagues them—even years after they have left the nest. People have a tendency to hold their loved ones to a standard of perfection not held for other relationships in their lives.

Many of us have a hard time remembering the fact that our parents and siblings are human beings, subject to the flaws and imperfections of the human race. We get stuck in past events where we felt a family member was rude, insensitive, selfish, preoccupied, unfair, or harsh. Repeating those events in our mental circuitry makes it impossible to let go and move on.

People who get in the habit of personalizing every inconsiderate thing that someone does… create a rigid mental program that continues to capture someone else's negativity, hold it in their own nervous system, and allow it to control their personal operating system.

Some family dynamics and interactions were painful when we experienced them. Oftentimes, they left us feeling unimportant, unloved, or insignificant. But as long as we continue to relive the negative experiences, run those negative thoughts, and feel the painful emotions that go with them, we cannot ever become our very best.

The problem with holding on to negative experiences and running the thoughts and emotions that go with them is that, at some level, you *believe* negative statements about yourself: the lies that you are unimportant, unlovable, and insignificant.

You have to be willing to dig deep and realize that no matter how terrible or hateful family members could be, they were acting out from the personal resources and mental programs they carried from their own upbringing. If your mother dealt with rejection or neglect as a child, from being raised by an alcoholic parent, chances are good that she was programmed by that rejection and pain and still carries her own sense of worthlessness. If you felt similar feelings of rejection and worthlessness from her, it was because she had no tools or understanding to heal herself and become a better parent to you. These family belief systems keep getting transferred to younger generations as long as they are not addressed and healed. You are the only one who can choose *now to* let negative family experiences go or to keep them alive in your life.

In the coaching process, it is both fascinating and astounding to see as we dissect the life story how irrational people's beliefs and thought patterns can be, especially concerning family dynamics. Usually, the person who is the most astounded with this discovery process is the one who is being coached. The realization and discovery that the beliefs and thought patterns (which have become their operating program) don't make any real sense anymore, bring about a huge sense of relief and freedom. Accepting the human flaws in their family members, and realizing that everyone is usually doing the best they can from their *own* (imperfect) state of consciousness is a big load off their shoulders. They can stop thinking that everything someone else does is about them. It is a magical moment when they realize much of the difficulty they've experienced in life is something formed and created in their own mind!

The giddiness they experience with this breakthrough comes from a sense of being freed from their own prison. They feel a little silly that they put themselves there and were under the illusion that someone from their upbringing was holding the key.

This releasing of blame and taking back responsibility for our life experience is the first healing component of our family history lesson. Whether our family members were supportive and nurturing or harsh and abusive, we can only experience real freedom to create our own lives, if we can learn to detach from the negative emotions and thought patterns that are based on old memories and perceptions. We sometimes think that harboring those painful memories and emotions gives us righteous justification to release the responsibility of our life's success. Often, people resort to blaming someone else for their lack of fulfillment because it absolves *them* of the responsibility to transform their lives. Transformation requires honesty, deliberate focus, and good old-fashioned hard work. Oftentimes, people shy away from owning their own life experience because it requires determination and action, which can be risky and demanding.

Your Family Is Great, But Who Are You?

The second healing component of our family history is to look at accepted family norms, beliefs, and values with fresh new vision. Many of us lock into habits that we're not even aware of, just because that is the way our families did things. Oftentimes, we can make a decision that doesn't honor our own heart's purpose because we know that our family doesn't find something acceptable. Family traditions and expectations, which sometimes go back for many generations, can feel excruciatingly punitive if your true vision of yourself and your life doesn't conform to accepted traditions and expectations.

There is the brilliant, creative young man, whose passion is theater and screen writing, but he succumbs to family pressure and chooses a finance major in college, because that is the area that the men in *his family* have achieved their success. He then spends the next twenty years hating his job and experiencing stress-related illness, because he denied his true calling and passion and did what others thought he *should* do.

There is the divorcee, who leaves an abusive marriage and finds a man of another ethnicity who is kind, caring, and successful. She finally relents to family pressure and breaks off the relationship because of the perceived "problems" in mixed-race marriages that her family has convinced her are inevitable. She spends the next ten years trying to find the love she felt (and then rejected) because someone else didn't think it was *right* for her.

Then there is the young man raised in poverty who has a brilliant mind and achieves superior academic success and scholarship opportunities… only to be mentally beaten down by family members, whose own insecurities won't let them accept a vision of one of their own becoming outstanding and successful, and transcending the life they've known for generations. He drops out of college, after starting, because he is worried about being rejected by his own family, and tries to prove to them he doesn't think he is better than they are.

Cherish the Good, Release the Rest

There are a lot of wonderful traditions and values we can take from our family experience, which will serve us as we move forward in our lives. But we must learn to step back and honestly observe our family experience, and the way those experiences have shaped and molded our perceptions, beliefs, values, and our self-worth. We can then decide what part of the family brain-mapping is getting us where we want to go, and what part is obsolete and needs to be modified. From there we choose which family values and beliefs support our own heart's knowing, and which ones do not.

When working with a client I use specific techniques for releasing negative family programming. In this releasing process, it is important to realize that there could be a wounded three-year-old, or five-year-old, or twelve-year-old inside of you. One of the processes I do in my work is to take someone back through their childhood, using hypnotherapy to heal the child at each stage, and to reintegrate those stages into a functional adult self. You may need to go back into your inner child, temporarily, and heal the hurt so that the adult in you can be in charge of your life, rather than the hurt child. A healed adult does a much better job of managing life's challenges.

The other part of this hypnotherapy healing session is to go to an offending family member (using the subconscious mind) and to offer forgiveness to him or her. Forgiveness doesn't ever mean you are condoning unacceptable behavior. It simply means that you understand people's shortcomings are usually a part of their own unhealed pain, and that you are willing to let go of the pain and resentment that would otherwise continue to poison your own health and well-being. Forgiving our family members, or anyone we feel has wronged us, is a crucial step to truly being free.

Your family history lesson is an important one. The journey, through your transformation, moves along more smoothly when you have taken the time to dissect and review the first conditioning to which you were exposed, to see how well it is serving you now. As you come to know your true self through this process, you can then determine what parts of it to release and what parts to hang on to and cherish, forever.

Chapter Five
Emotions: Your Mind/Body Connection

"The sorrow which has no vent in tears may make other organs weep."

—*Henry Maudsley*

❧

One of the most powerful ways I can help the people I see is to help them understand the wholeness of their entire person. In this chapter of our mind makeover, you will learn how thoroughly interconnected all parts of the mind and body are. In the past, science looked at the human body and mind as disconnected parts and separate systems, to be treated independently of each other. In more recent years, scientists have conducted fascinating research that now shows us just the opposite. We now know that the mind and body are interconnected in numerous ways through numerous systems. We know that the things we think, the emotions we feel, and the things we expose our bodies to, unquestionably affect our entire human organism and the way it presents itself in the world. There is no disconnection between thoughts, emotions, bodies, and environment. The only disconnection seems to be in our understanding of how integrated we truly are as humans, with a mind-body-spirit that operates as one.

How Is Everything That Happens in My Mind Connected to My Body?

Our brains as well as, quite frankly, our entire bodies are like their own little self-contained pharmacy. The brain, the glands, and the organs that reside in the systems throughout our bodies constantly secrete chemicals. These are released by a number of different triggers including our thoughts, our emotions, and environmental triggers like trauma, pollution, foods, and energy fields. These chemicals cause specific things to happen within the mind and the body, depending on which chemical was triggered and by what event.

Isn't This a Little "Woo-woo" and How Does It Help You Get What You Want in Life?

These chemical interactions and communications that take place constantly between your mind and body are helping to regulate your responses, choices, and actions in relationships and work. They also regulate your ability to be creative, dynamic, and to move forward. They help to coordinate various states of mind such as peace or discord, serenity or anxiety, depression or enthusiasm. These chemical messengers have the ability to block your immune system or enhance its strength. They are involved in production of energy and wellness in every system throughout your body.

Basically, nothing that takes place in your existence, as a human being, happens without the involvement of these little molecules of communication that run through our bodies delivering the messages, which are present in the thoughts and emotions that we think and feel each day. They are in charge of making sure that the signals from the mind are distributed to each of the cellular members of this community *called our body*. You might say their job is to make sure every cell in the body/mind community is on the same page.

Are You Crazy?

I remember that as a child, I would occasionally overhear my parents talking about Mrs. Such-and-such having an illness that someone had discovered was probably just psychosomatic. The way they pursed their lips and raised their brows when they said the word "psychosomatic" left me with the clear impression that the person they were referring to was slightly nuts. There was a clear implication that the illness was just a figment of Mrs. Such-and-such's imagination, and not real in any way.

If psychosomatic illness is an indication of mental lunacy then those of us who have ever been ill were slightly off our rockers. The word itself describes quite accurately the reality of most diseases and illness. *Psycho* means "Dealing with the mind" and *soma* means "body." Psychosomatic illness is an illness that's manifesting itself within the mind/body feedback loop. Science has proven that every illness, even those without a psychosomatic foundation has psychosomatic components. Later on, we'll discuss specific studies on disease or illness that is directly linked to a state of mind, including one on the common cold.

For now, let's just say that this new science has huge implications for your life and how you live it as it helps empower you to be more in control of your own health and states of well-being. Your state of being largely dictates how successful you will be in every area of your life and how much you will enjoy the life you live. When you can gain enough knowledge and understanding to begin to have more mastery over your states of being, you will have more mastery over your life.

So How Do Your Mind and Body "Talk"?

To understand clearly how all of this works, we have to get a little more scientifically technical. The growing fields of biomolecular science and neuroscience have provided us with so many exciting discoveries! These discoveries give us a clear picture of the interactions that happen between thoughts and emotions, and the chemical messengers acting within the systems in our bodies. The chemistry of human emotion seems to be the vehicle of communication between the mind and body.

Technically speaking, this is what's what. Our central nervous system is an extension of the brain, and runs through the entire body connecting all of the systems and various organs including the skin, through the peripheral nerves and neural circuitry. The nervous system is a regulator of all our bodily functions and systems including the respiratory, cardiovascular, endocrine, digestive, immune, and reproductive systems.

This hardwired system serves as an intricate network of pathways by which information, in the form of electrical impulses and ligands (chemical messengers), travels to pass along instructions to the various systems of our bodies. These messages journey from the brain to the body and back again. This activity is happening in every moment of our lives as we take in stimuli from our world. Much of what we take in is in the form of thoughts, which then pass through our perception filters, where they are transformed into our own personal representation of what just happened. That process activates chemicals, which begin to move throughout our minds and bodies to communicate the signals that just came from a thought, emotion, or feeling.

Recent discoveries show that memories are stored not only in the brain, but in a connected network throughout the body. A memory is nothing more than stored learned behavior. When we keep repeating thoughts or exist in a certain emotional state much of the time, our brains and bodies store this chemistry and its corresponding cell behaviors, which become "learned patterns" in our minds and bodies. Brain cells aren't the only ones that have the ability to hold memory. Cells throughout the body also have memory capability. Memories are constantly being transmitted through bundles of nerve cells that run all the way down the spinal cord and out into the organs, even reaching the skin's surface.

Ligands consist of neurotransmitters, steroids, and peptides. They are made up of amino acids or proteins. These chemicals move about through the brain and body seeking an appropriate place to dock within a cell, in order to share and communicate information. You might think of these molecules as little couriers picking up information and delivering it to even the outer reaches of the entire body. But the chemical information can't be received unless someone is there to sign for the package: a receptor molecule.

Receptor cells are single molecules that are attached to the surface of every cell in your body. Their job is to scan for information that is specifically meant for the type of cell they live on. Their function is to watch for the courier (ligand) with a message to come cruising by. The receptor cells dance around the surface membrane of each cell. They have roots that wind through the cell's membrane and penetrate deeply into its interior. They flutter around until the right chemical messenger—the one that is suitable for their cellular requirements—swims up to them and bind.

The Sex Your Cells Are Having May Be Producing Offspring You Don't Want!

In her book, *The Molecules of Emotion* (Scribner, 1997) molecular biologist Candace Pert, Ph.D. calls the peptide/receptor binding process "sex on a molecular level"![1] She describes how this binding causes the receptor molecule to move around and rearrange itself, until it transmits the new information from the ligand deep into the cell's surface. Immediately, a chain reaction of events takes place within the cell. These events could include decisions about cell division, adding or subtracting energetic chemical groups, or opening or closing ion channels found on cell membranes. These channels are like little valves, whose function is to control electrochemical balance by letting... say... a potassium ion to flow out, and an ion of sodium to flow in. All of these cellular events impact critical bodily functions like how the heart is beating.

Dr. Pert describes how the life of the cell and its behavior, at any given moment depends on which receptors are on its surface and whether or not they are occupied by ligands. Basically, the cell's performance, condition, and life expectancy are being determined by a symphony of events that is orchestrated through this constant communication process. Major physiological changes can be set into motion when one of these communication molecules locks onto a cell. This can then translate into huge changes in physical state and levels of activity, moods and attitudes, and behaviors.

In the earlier days of receptor molecule research, scientists thought that emotions were found exclusively in the more primitive part of the brain; an area that includes the amygdala, the limbic cortex, and the hippocampus. They called this area of the brain the "seat of emotions." Now we know that the hippocampus might actually serve as a gateway for all emotional experience. Scientists have found traces of virtually every emotional receptor peptide in the hippocampus.

As a result of more extensive research that has gone on, we now know that the receptors for "emotion peptides" are also in place throughout the body... running down the spine on both sides and within the organs that the nervous system connects to. Dr. Pert coined the term *neuropeptide* to refer to these chemical messengers that appear in all the systems of our bodies, as the physical manifestations of our emotions.

The autonomic nervous system is integral to the emotional peptide connection. The implications are tremendous considering the autonomic nervous system's job is to act as the control system of the body. This regulating of heart rate, digestion, respiration, salivation, perspiration, urination, and sexual arousal are all performed primarily without any conscious control or sensation. The evidence of emotion peptides within the system suggests that even our autonomic patterns are emotionally encoded.

In the modern world, people are commonly afflicted with ailments, such as digestive issues, atrial fibrillation of the heart, and erectile dysfunction or low libido—all functions that rely on the autonomic nervous system. These are just a few of the disorders that could be manifesting as a result of emotional stresses, or states that often go unacknowledged. When you consider the insatiable demands of most of our lifestyles, it is not surprising that our emotions get pushed aside and buried. We often simply don't have the time or the ability to deal with them. It's no wonder then that emotional residue ends up getting stuck throughout our bodies, where it creates havoc within the systems we rely on to maintain our health and wellness.

There are concentrated clusters of nerves very near each other in locations throughout the body in which neuropeptide receptors are highly concentrated. These areas called "nodal points" are present in all the sites in which sensory information—sight, sound, smell, taste, and touch enter into the nervous system. Nodal points are positioned in the body, so that they can be easily accessed by virtually all neuropeptides (different ones at different times), and so that vast amounts of information can be communicated. Depending on which neuropeptide is occupying the receptors of a particular nodal point, the information the receptors carry modulates certain neurophysiological changes. They can cause a switch from a physiological sensation to an emotional experience from the same nodal point. The changes can take place at the unconscious level or be switched to top conscious priority… based on which neuropeptide is the occupier of the receptors at the time.

EFT, the energy therapy that I often integrate into my sessions is based on accessing these nodal points of the body through a protocol of tapping on meridian lines to discharge emotional chemistry that has become "stuck." For an instruction manual on EFT go to: **www.crystaldwyer.com/eft.html**.

Some Fascinating Studies…

Dr. Robert Ader wrote *Psychoneuroimmunology* (Elsevier Academic Press, 2007), the first book in a new field of science in 1981. In it, he explained that the psyche controls the cells of the body including the immune system.

In 1974, Dr. Ader had stumbled upon one of his first important discoveries when he was conducting an experiment to investigate how long a conditioned response (Pavlov's concept) might last in rats. He combined saccharine water and the nausea-inducing drug, Cytoxan, to train the rats to associate the sweet water with a bellyache. Afterwards, he gave them only the sweet water without the nausea drug to see how long they would continue to associate the two. The rats unexpectedly began to fall prey to disease and to die off. A confused Ader checked the properties of the nausea drug and found that one of its side effects was as an immune suppressant. Even though the rats no longer received the immune-suppressing nausea drug and had only received it for a short time, their minds linked the sweet water to the immune shutdown. Essentially, the *expected* response in the rats' minds is what caused them to become sick and die.[2]

A provocative study done by Harvard Psychologist, Ellen Langer, Ph.D., tested if our perception of how much exercise we are getting has any affect on how our bodies look. Her research studied hotel maids. She found that most of the maids didn't see themselves as physically active, even though they lugged vacuums and carts around and spent almost every moment of their days in physical activity. Sixty-seven percent said they didn't regularly exercise; one-third claimed they got no exercise at all. As bizarre as their perception of their lack of activity was, even more strange was the fact that none of the women's bodies seemed to benefit from their daily physical activity, even though it far exceeded the U.S. Surgeon General's recommendation.

Langer divided the group in two. Half were informed that their daily activity exceeded the Surgeon General's definition of an active lifestyle. The others were told nothing. One month later the science team returned to find that the group who had been educated had a decrease in their blood pressure, weight, and waist-to-hip ratio. What Langer's team witnessed was a definite placebo effect in which the women's mental perceptions about their fitness caused a marked change in their bodies' form and function.[3]

Compelling studies have also been done on the link between depression and various diseases. Here are some of the intriguing results.

- People with depression are four and a half times more likely to suffer a heart attack. Depressed people who do suffer a heart attack have three times the risk of death than those who aren't depressed.[4]

- Patients who were chronically depressed for six years had an 88 percent greater risk of developing cancer over the next 4 years.[5]

- Depressed people are more vulnerable to Type 2 diabetes.[6]

- Children with anxiety and depression need more medications, and spend more time in the hospital than those who are more emotionally stable. Emotional stress also seems to be a big trigger for the onset of asthma and asthma attacks.[7]

- Patients who started out with normal blood pressure were monitored for sixteen years. Those who suffered from anxiety and depression, at the start of the study, were two to three times more likely to develop hypertension (high blood pressure).[8]

These studies all indicate a direct link between a state of mind, such as depression and the resulting effect it has on the physical wellness.

More of Dr. Pert's research shows that the common cold virus (Rheovirus) uses the same cell receptors that Norepinephrine does to invade a cell.[9] Norepinephrine is the informational substance that flows when a person is happy. This probably accounts for why happier people get sick less often. The cell receptor is full of the happy substance and not available for the Rheovirus to dock on.

In June 2008, Ephraim C. Trakhtenberg published an article in the International Journal of Neuroscience called, *The Effects of Guided Imagery and the Immune System*. It describes the research that was done using guided imagery as a means of altering the immune system. The study showed that guided imagery can reduce stress, elevate the immune system, and that cell-specific imagery positively affected white blood cell counts. The results were so compelling that ongoing studies have already been planned.[10]

Science Leaves Us No Reason to Doubt

There are hundreds of studies that I could cite to demonstrate the myth-breaking work in the major areas of science that is concerned with the where, why, and what of a healthy, balanced human organism. The fields of endocrinology, neuroscience, and immunology can no longer avoid the reality of our connected human mind/body system, with its overlapping communication networks and continuous integration of information. The closer science looks at this connection the more it discovers the linkage of every part of our mind, body, and spirit.

Everything we think, feel, and do, and everything that goes into our bodies from our breakfast choice to what kinds of chemicals enter our system through pesticides, pollution, water quality, and the medications we use will impact how we feel, behave, and how our bodies will perform. All of these things shape what we call our life. Fortunately, because of the constant ability for our bodies to receive new information and learn new things, our state of health or well-being isn't fixed or static.

If in the past, you were living in a negative emotional and mental state and didn't pay attention to what went into your body... recognize that it is never too late to make changes. In subsequent chapters we will explore how you can intervene on behalf of your own long-term health and state of well-being. Through awareness and intention, you can change the dynamic flow of information and energy that courses through your body/mind. You can learn and practice the techniques, and make choices that will help you create and maintain the states of being you desire.

Where Do You Get on Board to Change This Ongoing Feedback Cycle of Your Mind and Body?

The answer to the preceding question is: anywhere. Since the mind and body constantly communicate and feed information to each other, at whatever point you decide to intervene, your intervention will affect the other parts of the loop.

This is what I love about the many alternative therapies that are available, today. People report how they get great results for everything, from stress reduction to pain alleviation using therapies ranging from acupuncture, massage, energy healing, emotional therapy, hypnosis, meditation, homeopathy, and naturopathy. Naysayers often question the credibility of these methods, sometimes for the very reason that they all seem to bring some relief or benefit to the participant. They question the veracity of such a diverse array of therapies being able to target a problem or issue in completely different ways; yet, both practitioner and patient claim that they work.

In other words, how could all these techniques be effective if they are coming from such different approaches? I mean... lying there with needles hanging out of your skin (acupuncture) is a far different approach than having someone put you in a recliner and talk you into a subconscious trance, while reframing your subconscious thought programs to the ones you desire (hypnotherapy). Yet, both of these therapies have been remarkably successful for such issues as baby conception, anxiety, chronic pain, and peak performance just to name a few.

These diverse therapies can all claim results because they all are intervening in the mind/body feedback loop. They simply have different entry points. All of them work because of the fabulous communication system we have inside us, which enables our entire system to share information including thought changes, emotional changes, energy changes, and chemical changes that come from such things as vitamin supplements and dietary modifications.

I get tremendous satisfaction from having trained in several different therapies because it allows me to help my clients to access the mind/body feedback loop from a variety of angles. For therapies I don't cover, I often refer clients to other practitioners, such as naturopathic physicians, chiropractors, and acupuncturists. Oftentimes, taking a multilevel approach helps resolve problems faster because the wellness loop is being entered at multiple portals.

The scientific knowledge we now have about our mind/body connection gives us amazing opportunities in our lives. This awareness provides the ability to tune in and to take the steps needed to intervene (whenever necessary) to create unprecedented levels of health, happiness, and well-being for ourselves and the people we love.

Part Two

The Seven Pillars of Transformation

❧

For the second section of this life transformation manual, I am providing you with a set of solid yet simple concepts that you can easily refer back to as you continue to grow and move forward in your journey. In the Introduction, I talked about the specific set of principles that I developed through my trials and tribulations, and ultimately my victories. Those principles that kept guiding me to greater levels of success and happiness became the Seven Pillars of Transformation for this book, which you will learn in Part Two.

Definitions for the word *pillar* include "tower of strength" and "source of strength." As you rid yourself of *messy thinking* and begin to construct a new foundation for clear, productive thinking, these seven principles or *pillars* will act as a source of strength on which your life transformation will be built. Whenever new challenges come forth in your life… returning to these pillars will allow you to ground yourself in basic essential truths, so that you can continue to move forward, again and again.

Chapter Six
The First Pillar: Self-honesty

"Honesty is the first chapter of Book of Wisdom."
—Thomas Jefferson

Self-honesty is a crucial pillar in the construction of a clear thinking mind. In the process of working with clients to help them overcome issues, I've found that those who have the greatest capacity for being *completely honest* with themselves... break through barriers and move forward the fastest. The coaching process requires revealing yourself to yourself (and hopefully to your life coach, if you have one). We automatically feel vulnerable when we have to admit our fears, insecurities, and other negative emotions we've all experienced, such as jealousy and resentment. We're usually very good at presenting a certain picture of ourselves that masks the qualities we think are less than desirable.

This can be different for everyone... depending on his or her own perception of what an acceptable emotional trait is for him or her personally. A man, for instance may have a hard time admitting he is afraid. In his belief system feeling or showing fear indicates weakness. On the other hand, he may be very willing to put on a tough-guy, anger façade to disguise the fear he is *really* living with. A woman may be carrying intense anger and resentment, but feigning agreeability and putting on the facade of being extremely sweet. Her belief system might be telling her that attractive, desirable women must be sweet and not angry or aggressive.

Those Sneaky Egos

Our ego-selves do a good job of creating all kinds of facades for us to hide behind. An insecure person sometimes masks his or her insecurity by being a chronic smartass. A woman who's always felt socially-inferior has a rigid standard of only allowing herself to buy high-priced designer clothing, even when she really can't afford designer wear. A man who was considered wimpy as a youth works out obsessively and takes steroids to mask the insecurity (he still feels) that was never healed. A woman who lacks the confidence to take the risk to be in a relationship with a man becomes hypercritical of all men. Her *I-Hate-Men* facade disguises the fear and lack of confidence she has about putting herself out there and risking rejection.

In an effort to avoid feeling exposed and defenseless, our ego designs itself as a cloak that shrouds our greatest fears and weaknesses. Every one of us has worn a facade or two that has kept us from revealing our true selves. It is a difficult thing for us to lose this mask that we have learned to count on so that our worst remains unseen. We think that if we drop the façade we lose part of ourselves, and it feels scary. The truth is that we *do* lose a part of ourselves, but the piece we lose is a piece of the ego-self that has outlived its useful purpose.

My Personal Story of Ego Shedding

I can personally attest to the power of this process because it has happened to me plenty of times in my life. Like the time a few years ago, my then twelve-year-old daughter developed a frightening eating disorder. This was a little girl who had always been on the thin side. Since I had always been concerned about her eating enough it felt as if my worst nightmare was coming true. Our emotions are powerful teachers, which is why I believe God gives them to us. The debilitating worry and fear I felt were the catalysts that helped me recognize the changes I needed to make. The part of my ego-self that had to die was the one who had created an identity around the story, "My kids are perfect and don't have problems like other people's children." That phony part of me had to go, in order for me really to be able to help my beautiful daughter.

The new me that took her place from the ashes is a much-improved model. This one says, "My children have the right to experience their own struggles and challenges so that they may grow from them and evolve. My job is to love and support them through it without my ego becoming attached."

I'm happy to say my daughter has recovered. Through a commitment to her own inner work she has become her healthy, confident self once again. But two important pieces of the healing puzzle lay with her father and me. It took a lot of self-honesty to face how we could have been contributing to the destructive cycle our daughter was caught in. One of the things I needed to get in touch with was the "my-kids-are-perfect" ego-self of mine, which developed from a chronic fear I used to carry about all of the bad things that *could* happen to my wonderful kids. I was so worried about the potential pitfalls that were out there for kids, that I needed to believe my kids were above such things. Without realizing it I was projecting this constant worry onto them, which in my younger daughter's case contributed to her anxiety and control issues.

Just as I had to release my attachment to perfection, my husband had to release the part of his ego-self that believed he needed to have ultimate control and the last say in all family matters. He learned how to honor everyone's feelings and input, even if he didn't necessarily agree with it all the time. This *I-control-everything* bully in him had to die for this new, better man to live.

This experience, which none of us would have asked for, ended up being a redemptive force for our entire family. Situations like this work like a swarm of bees that flies up your pant leg. There is no way to hold still and avoid dealing with them. You continue to feel pain and discomfort until you do. By allowing ourselves to be vulnerable, and incorporating our own self-honesty into the healing process, we released some of our most destructive facades, and the debilitating fears that kept them alive.

During periods of our most difficult challenges, when we're facing life-altering consequences, an opportunity surfaces to release that which isn't real and to embrace what is. Letting go of the counter-productive parts of the ego allows our most authentic selves an opportunity to shine through. We've all looked at an old photograph and wondered to ourselves how we ever could have thought that old hairstyle looked *good* on us. Of course fashions change. But it's also like we wore our hair one way for so long that we couldn't really see it any more. Our outdated ego-parts are much the same. We get used to them and don't really notice them anymore, unless something causes us to change them. Then we realize how not-so-pretty they were and wonder why we wore them.

In my case, the choice to let go of my perceived need to appear as a perfect mother with perfect kids came about from my deep, authentic love for my daughter. That was the driving force that made me get out there, talk to people, and seek the best care for her. My love for her and my desire to see her well… freed me from some of my own deep insecurities and brought about my own transformation. Better than a brand-new hair-do!

The Greatest You Is Waiting to Come Out

The greatest life you can live is the one in which you die and are reborn many times over. It is never the real self (the soul-self) that dies. Rather, it is different versions of the ego-self, which were poised to really mess things up if they didn't get out of the way.

If you are in your forties or fifties *now* imagine if you had the exact same ego-self you had in you twenties. Or if you are in your twenties imagine if you had your ten-year-old ego-self. Perhaps you *do* know someone who still operates through life with his or her child ego-self in charge. If so, you will often feel like you're dealing with an unreasonable child when interacting with this person. In some ways you are. People who suffer traumatic events or intense stress or pressure (at certain ages of childhood development) will become emotionally stuck at that stage of emotional development. Even though they become educated and successful in certain areas of their lives, they will still revert to childish or adolescent patterns of processing change, conflict, and emotional issues, especially in close relationships.

When I'm helping someone who is still letting his or her child-self run the show, emotionally, I do some intensive work through hypnotherapy... regressing them back to those young ages where the trauma was experienced, and where they began those initial emotional and thought patterns that are preventing them from existing in a relationship as a functional adult. We use a technique of comforting the hurting child at the critical ages and events where the trauma occurred, and then we reframe creating a healthy scenario; where the adult-self relieves the child of his or her responsibility to run the show. This allows the adult-self to step in and take over. It is through the client's acceptance of his or her own vulnerabilities that a much stronger version of the person comes forth.

Donna's Story

Donna came to me as a divorced mother with two children. She wanted so many things for herself but couldn't seem to feel any satisfaction or fulfillment, and she had no idea why. During the intake process it became apparent that Donna had been using her "story" for a very long time as a means to assign blame to her mother, her father, her ex-husband, and her boyfriend. She was angry and disgusted at all of them for not being enough and not doing enough, so that she could have the life she felt she deserved.

As we began to process her life using the self-honesty principle, we rooted out the truth about how jealous she was of many of her friends, who it seemed to her were always getting so much more. Their husbands were better catches. They had nicer cars, better vacations, nicer homes, and even second homes in exciting, wonderful places. All of these were things that she had decided she deserved long ago, which she had never gotten. What really pained her was that she had gone to college with some of these people, and had run in the same social circles as they had. She wondered what in the world had gone wrong for her.

It was apparent to me after a session or two, that Donna was operating emotionally as an entitled, spoiled child. She had grown up with a mother, whose primary focus was material wealth and a country-club lifestyle. Her mother had left her father for a much richer man. The mental and emotional programming Donna had developed (over the years) was that material wealth made you more valuable and loveable. The little girl inside of her still felt the same pain and inadequacy, from the conditions her mother placed on her love for Donna, and on all of her important relationships. Because that little-girl part of her was never healed, she still responded in the same childish or adolescent way she always had to life's challenges: by throwing a tantrum and blaming everyone around her for not filling her needs. She had never learned to base her love for herself or others on the inner qualities that really make someone who they are. The childhood programming was always telling her that you measure a person based on what material things they have.

In our sessions, we worked on healing the child inside that never really felt valued for who she was. During her sessions, we also went through a subconscious forgiveness process that allowed Donna to understand how her parents' upbringings had contributed to their limitations in being parents to her. Forgiving them included cutting the emotional cord that was causing Donna to act like an irrational child in her life as an adult. After she did this she could see how blaming everyone for her lack had gotten her nowhere.

The next thing we worked on was establishing new values and rules about people's worth and the qualities that make a person great. She learned that the reason all of the riches she coveted had eluded her was that she had been focusing on the riches, and failing to see that usually people with strong character, discipline, and honesty are the ones who can achieve great things including material abundance. We did reinforcement exercises, to refocus her attention on the value and richness of the inner qualities of a person.

After four or five sessions, Donna looked, felt, and acted like a new person. Her anxiety about not being good enough was greatly diminished. She felt like she was *truly* enjoying the people and the moments of her life, and she stepped up to her responsibility for her own fulfillment. She started looking for a good job in which she could put her own talents to work and create abundance in her life, instead of sitting around waiting for someone to bestow it upon her.

The process that unfolded sometimes took a great deal of brutal self-honesty on Donna's part. She had worn her façade so well, for so long. Reaching this level of truth within her and moving forward with it has truly changed her life *forever*.

Be Your Best Friend, Not Your Worst Enemy

My own journey of self-honesty has been long and painful at times. On a scale of authenticity, the woman my husband married twenty years ago bears little resemblance to the one he's married to today. I spent years peeling away the layers that disguised this more authentic version of me. Those multiple layers were there, so that even I would not have to face my fears of not being good enough. The mask I wore was one of perfection. Inside, I was terribly afraid that I would be found lacking in virtually everything I did. In the meals I faithfully prepared; in the home I carefully decorated; in the way I dressed; in the things I said, and even in the way I nurtured my children; I was on guard.

My armor of perfection was so excruciatingly tight, that it left little room for me to take a breath and enjoy the small yet rich experiences I was a part of. Much of the time, my anxiety over an inferior performance (at any little thing about my parenting) robbed me of the type of joyful moments that come from just going with the flow. Looking back, I realize that my children would be just as healthy and happy, today, if I had given in to the occasional urge to serve frozen waffles for dinner after a non-stop exhausting day; instead of torturing my worn-out, frazzled self into producing a perfectly balanced, well-prepared meal that no one scrutinizing good parenting tactics could find fault with.

There was little room under my perfection disguise to be kind to myself. For a long time, I forgot how. Yet, the only thing that made me continually beat myself up was my own fear of inadequacy. The side effect of this rigidly perfectionist ego-self was resentment, which arose when my self-sacrificing efforts would go unnoticed or unappreciated. As I punished myself into perfection each day, I needed to know from my significant loved ones, mainly my husband and children, that my efforts were just as important to them as they were to my desperately hungry ego.

Through the years, God just kept showering little opportunities down on me in the form of epiphanies, challenges, heartaches, and glorious victories that allowed me to change my thoughts and perceptions and to change my ways. I look back and feel sorry for that wound-up person that I was, so often. I am so very thankful for every little experience (good and bad) that brought me to the place I'm at *now* in my journey. It feels so good to embrace my authentic self. It feels so good to admit I'm not perfect and I don't have to be. It feels so good to know that I'm still loveable and valuable (even with my imperfections) and that sometimes it's my worst qualities that end up teaching me how to be my best.

Processing your life through the Pillar of Self-honesty reveals monsters of fear, inadequacy, resentment, jealousy, and hopelessness. Allowing a phony ego-self to camouflage scary little creatures only feeds their hungry appetite, and creates even bigger monsters. I've dealt with clients, whose fear of their darker qualities has caused them to bury their little demons so deeply, and hide them so carefully that they have finally become raging beasts. When these people come to me, it is in a state of desperation brought about by their inability to thrive or function in *any* relationship with anyone. Their inability to reach in and unmask their greatest fears and weaknesses, even to themselves, has led to repetitious cycles of dysfunction in relationships that begin to resemble insanity.

My key strategy, in helping someone at that level, is to tap into his or her fears. Using a process of questioning and EFT, we hack away at their ego-fortress until their emotions cause a break in the wall they've erected. We keep chipping away using reminder statements about loving themselves, even though they have these negative emotions.

The relief that is felt when the wall can come down, the monsters can all come out, and we can see that they're not so scary in the light of day is immeasurable. This becomes the starting point to living life as his or her authentic self—fully human, fully flawed, and fully perfect all at the same time.

Finding the authentic self, through self-honesty, is in essence rediscovering our own soul. When we apply the self-honesty principle, things will begin to rapidly shift in our own lives and the lives of those we interact with. Imagine how different things would be, if we felt truly free to live honestly and to express ourselves honestly in all our relationships. This is not to say that if someone is wearing clothing we don't like, we must blurt out our opinion and hurt his or her feelings. It is about conveying a true expression of the things that really matter. Often, we avoid taking an honest look at ourselves because we immediately start to judge ourselves or feel self-hatred, when we acknowledge a weakness or fault in ourselves. Staying neutral and avoiding any kind of self-judgment in the self-honesty process is so very important to its success. The following key points will provide a structure for you to integrate the self-honesty pillar into your life.

The Key Points of the Self-honesty Principle

It is helpful to write these key points down and post them in a place where it is easy to see them throughout the day. They will become healthy reminders to keep returning to self-honesty, until it becomes a more natural habit.

- Be willing to look at yourself with complete love and forgiveness. Honestly acknowledge what is happening within you, without self-judgment.

- Be fearless in communicating what you are feeling without complicating it with insults, judgments, or accusations.

- Take responsibility for what you are feeling. No one can *make* you feel something. You are feeling something and reacting in a certain way primarily because of your own filters and perceptions. If someone has been harsh or rude tell him or her you felt they were being harsh or rude.

- Don't feel obligated to say something if you can't be completely honest, or if you need more time to think about the best way to handle something. We often feel like we always need a response, comeback, or defense when something comes at us.

- Don't react verbally from a negative emotional state. If you know you can't give an honest, authentic reply, simply say that you really aren't feeling this is the right time to respond or talk about the given subject. Then, take some time to sort through your thoughts and feelings, so that what eventually comes out of your mouth is honest, clear, sincere communication.

If you must deal with someone in your life that is over-the-top with anger, demands, or inappropriate behavior toward you set proper boundaries to give yourself distance from that person's energy. Step up and honestly say, "The way you are behaving right now is *not* okay with me, and I won't be able to talk about this unless it is done with mutual respect." Then remove yourself from the situation until such time as you are comfortable that respectful conversation can happen.

Living more honestly is essential to becoming the greatest version of you. When you begin to be more honest with yourself and others, it becomes more natural to expect the same from those in your life. Living more authentically, is truly the way to begin to rid yourself of the ego-parts of you that are keeping you from being in alignment with your true soul. This is why the self-honesty pillar is the first in my transformational program. This has to happen before anything else can.

CHAPTER SEVEN

The Second Pillar: Observation

"People's minds are changed through observation and not through argument."
—*Will Rogers*

⚜

To transform your life, you must become an observer. When you begin to practice the art of observation at multiple levels, your feelings about yourself and your interactions with others will change drastically and immediately. The ability to observe your world (and your interaction within it) puts you in a posture to respond objectively and deliberately to life, rather than snapping into automatic emotional, thought, and behavioral responses.

Observation is an essential step toward lasting change because to change something, you must first be able to carefully notice the way it is now. Observation allows us the chance to step out of our routine. When we are perfectly honest, we know there are many times we fall back on pre-programmed responses without really noticing what we're doing and the effect it has on our lives. The implementation of observation in your life will provide you open portals from which multiple paths of your choosing emerge. There are three areas in which we *must* become experts in observation to truly transform.

First Observation Skill Is to Observe Your Own Thoughts

The first area in which we must become proficient in the art of observation is in *the practice of observing our thoughts.* In the thoughts chapter, we discussed how people become confused and begin to think they are their thoughts. We now know that we can notice our thoughts, observe our thoughts, and change our thoughts at will. Pausing to become an observer of your own thoughts and perceptions will put you at the very gateway of profound life change. The observation process is the catalyst for learning to separate from what is running through our minds.

I want you to try a little exercise, right now. Read through the instructions once. Then do the process. You're going to do this exercise with your eyes closed.

Thought Observation Exercise

After closing your eyes take a few deep breaths and try to think of nothing. Think of yourself as an entity apart from anything that runs through your mind. If a thought pops into your mind observe it in a detached way, as if it is just a leaf drifting past you in the wind. It is not connected to you in any way. Make sure you don't judge or respond to your thoughts in any way. Continue to sit quietly for a few minutes observing your thoughts and detaching from them as you let them blow by. After you've done this for a couple of minutes keeping your eyes closed, just ask yourself the question, "Who is watching these thoughts that drift though my mind?" Listen and watch for an answer.

When you feel ready open your eyes.

Your observer is the part of you who is able to look at your own thoughts and realize the separateness between you and your thoughts. Your observer is your higher self—your soul self—the part of you who is actually able to notice when you are feeling, saying, or doing something without subjectivity. We've all had moments after we've said or done something and noticed a voice within us saying, "I'm surprised I just said that," or "I really don't know why I'm doing this." This wonderful part of who we are is our essential soul-self. The true essential-self observes without judgment. This part of you, somehow, is always more in tune and more aligned with your greatest being, your greatest potential, and the essence of God around you and within you than is the ego-self.

Discovering the observer part of you is a seemingly magical experience. When you tap into the observer inside of you and begin to understand the separateness between you and your thoughts, then you will understand that your thoughts, perceptions, and the beliefs that you've formed from them don't necessarily have to be there. If you can separate from your thoughts then why should you keep the thought patterns that are causing you grief and misery?

The observer-you has a naturally discriminating palate. Like a seasoned taster of fine foods, it inherently recognizes behaviors and attitudes that are less than palatable to your essential soul-self. The more you employ the expertise of your observer, the more adept your observer will become at revealing the quality of your thoughts and behaviors. As a food taster has no reason to be angry or ashamed of the foods tried that are less than palatable (the taster simply ceases to eat unpleasant foods), so too, your observer can learn to notice behaviors and attitudes without responding to them with emotion, but allowing you to simply not choose them anymore.

Observe and Then Ask the Questions

So once you grasp the concept of observation where do you go with it? How can observing reality with neutrality become a stepping-stone in your transformation? Here's how. Each day as you go about processing your daily interactions and experiences, when you find yourself feeling anger, turmoil, or confusion or if you're having a difficult time with someone stop yourself in that moment, take a deep breath, and let your observer ask:

- What thoughts am I thinking, right now, about this experience?

- What emotions am I feeling, right now, about this situation and why?

- What beliefs are behind these emotions?

- What are the automatic negative thoughts that are popping up and why?

After you've paused to observe the thought process cycling through your mind, at that moment, the next step is to ask what I call the *challenge questions,* which are:

- Are my perceptions accurate, or are they just my way of seeing things through my previous conditioning or biases?

- Is the belief that is bringing up turmoil, right now, based on non emotionally-charged perceptions and truth, or is it loaded with baggage that doesn't serve my highest good?

- Are the values I'm assigning to this situation prioritized using the truth of my highest self?

- Am I recognizing that the negative emotions I'm experiencing, right now, may be due to old thought programming that I can release now?

As turmoil, stress, or negative feelings come up stop and observe your thoughts and emotions. Then use these challenge questions. You will actually be *challenging* the thought patterns that cause negative emotions, which may have been hanging around far too long. Like finally realizing you can jump off a merry-go-round when you feel dizzy and you aren't able to focus; you can suddenly step back from the motion of the thoughts and emotions that keep going round and round in your mind. You naturally possess this ability.

Emotional patterns and thought patterns gain momentum after being pushed along enough times. Getting out of the momentum by stepping back from it lets you see those patterns for what they are. Many could be responsible for making you feel frustrated, defeated, sad, or sick in the past. To change your life and transform, you must get in touch with what you are doing that isn't working for you, or is even working *against* you.

I recommend writing the challenge questions down and posting them on the wall near your desk, putting them in your PDA, or keeping them with you in your wallet. It is also helpful to write down the answers you receive, if you can, especially in the beginning stages of your mind makeover. Writing down things you learn about yourself is a crucial part of your transformational process. The process of writing uses several channels of sensory input, so it really helps you to *learn* about the mental programs that get in the way of your happiness and success. Whenever issues come up, referring back to the things you are learning about yourself, through your past note-taking, will help you form permanent habits of challenging that which is no longer working in your life.

A Little Girl's Epiphany on Observation

When I was seven years old, my family took our first trip to Hawaii. My parents put five kids (the final four had not been born yet, although it is evident from the videos that Mom was carrying number six underneath her maternity bathing suit) on a Pan Am Airline flight, and we landed on the beautiful island of Oahu. As a girl used to the dry, cold, high-plain winds of Southeastern Idaho, I remember thinking that I'd never felt anything so delicious as the warm, moist breezes and the warm, gentle rain when I first felt them, as I walked across the tarmac to the airline terminal.

After we got to our hotel, the first thing on our agenda was to play in the ocean. We all raced out and started frolicking in the water laughing and shouting in our excitement. I had been too young to spend much time in the ocean when we had visited California a few times before, so my experience with ocean tides was limited. Then it happened. I got in trouble. Suddenly, as I was standing in water up to my armpits looking toward the beach and calling out to one of my siblings, a wave much bigger than the ones I had paddled along with, so far, grabbed me from behind, pulled me down in a forward roll, and shot me all the way to the beach like a little bowling ball being thrown for a strike. After what felt like forever, on the last couple of rolls, I felt my back scratch against the sand as I was eventually rolled into the shallow water.

I scrambled to get my footing in the sand and water, sputtering and choking… feeling really, really mad. My mom, with intuitive timing, turned her head in my direction right then and with a quizzical look asked me if I was okay. I nodded, barely, and marched straight to my towel and sat down. Mom knew not to ask anything else for the time being. As I sat there staring at the kids *still* in the water and *still* having fun I said to myself, "I hate the ocean and I'm never going in it, again."

Then I kept staring at the ocean, looking at the kids, and thinking to myself, "How did I get caught up in the force of the ocean like that and not know what had happened to me?" I was angry because I had been completely overtaken by its force. I was watching my siblings play and trying to notice what I had missed. The longer I watched, the more I noticed the pattern of the waves coming and going. I noticed that kids would turn away from the beach *toward* the oncoming waves, so they knew when to expect them. When the wave got closer, the kids would paddle *with* the wave and the wave would *lift* them up instead of pulling them down. In this way they would have a thrilling ride into the beach on *top* of the wave.

The longer I sat and *observed* the waves and the riders, the more I realized that if I had done this to begin with I wouldn't have hated the ocean. I would have understood the ebb and flow, and I would have known how to ride with the wave instead of being blind-sided by it. I wouldn't have been taken under, if I had first just observed what was really going on. If seven-year-olds can have epiphanies this was certainly one of those moments for me. I forgave the ocean and raced back in to have fun, knowing that if I didn't want to feel so helpless, all I had to do was watch and notice.

Observation can bring us epiphanies. Pulling back and looking at what is really going on gives us the space to see things more clearly and objectively. The drama and power of life often resembles the ocean. If we keep throwing ourselves into it and never stop to observe what is happening—if we never really notice the ebb and flow, the rhythm, or the inherent power of life—we can be sucked under and thrown around without ever understanding what happened or why. If we take certain moments to pull out, to step back from the drama and power, and to observe what is going on then we can jump back in, enthusiastically, and with a renewed sense of power and awareness.

Observing your state of mind as it unfolds throughout the day; then answering the challenge questions as you experience different states… will provide guidance to you about the truth behind your experience of life, so far. When you see the truth in your answers, it will point you away from inaccurate perceptions, biases, and conditioning.

Your answers will assist you in unloading the emotional baggage, that you now know *isn't* serving you, in becoming the greatest version of yourself that you can be. Honestly answering the challenge questions will help you realize that some of the things you have valued the most, until now, weren't prioritized using the truth of your highest self. They will cause you to recognize that you can now release the old thought programs, which were triggered and reinforced by negative emotions.

When you first begin to practice the art of observation, you may occasionally hear your observer defending actions or behaviors that are less than palatable, and citing some really good justifications for them. Don't fall for it. That's your ego posing as a neutral observer. Simply tell it to go back to bed and let your true observer do its job, which is helping you to see your behaviors and attitudes, clearly, and if they support or defeat you.

Defensiveness Provides the Clue

The more closely you examine your emotionally charged reactions, the more you will hone in on the flawed and outdated beliefs that are causing them. Defensiveness is a prime indicator that a negative self-belief, such as unworthiness or inadequacy is lurking below in your subconscious mind.

When your proverbial buttons get pushed, triggered emotions surge up and snap, like a deep-water shark that's been disturbed. If you find yourself being defensive during interactions with those around you... drawing upon the principle of self-honesty (see Chapter 6) stop right then, and let your *observer* ask what is really going on with the situation. Use the challenge questions to get to the bottom of your defensiveness.

Going through this exercise, whenever you feel defensive, will help you get in touch with the emotions behind the defensiveness. In later chapters, we will learn about using our emotions and feelings to accelerate healing and success in our lives. We'll see that if something isn't working in our lives, it doesn't necessarily mean we are making bad choices. It means we are basing our perceptions and choices on bad information that somehow got locked into our mind programs. Observation causes us to stop and review the program itself, and to change or replace it with better, updated information.

Second Observation Skill: Neutral Observation of Events

We've covered the first area of observation, which is the observation of your own thoughts and perceptions. Now we'll move to the second area of observation that you must practice, in order to achieve emotional and mental freedom. This is about learning to accurately observe the events that are unfolding around you. The objective here is to understand the difference between observation and *evaluation*.

Until we learn the art of observation, most of us reactively evaluate a situation rather than simply observe it. Evaluation requires an interpretation, which is done through our own subjective mental filters followed by a judgment, which is a decision about whether something is good or bad. If you can learn to describe what actually happened, rather than depending on your interpretation when dealing with an event, you will avoid so much unnecessary conflict. If you want to be an objective observer it is wise to ask yourself:

- What actually happened here?

- What did you actually see or hear in regards to this occurrence?

- Are you responding to what you actually saw or heard or to something inside of you?

When you have an emotional response to an event, the situation can deteriorate very quickly. If you find yourself reacting, emotionally, pause in that very moment and determine the difference between your judgment of the event and a purely *objective observation* of what just happened. Objectivity gives us the clarity we need to recognize how much we are reacting, emotionally, to a situation based on our interpretation.

This process becomes empowering because it causes us to realize that we have the power to prevent a false interpretation. It is often these false interpretations of events that have kept us locked into emotional pain. That pain can go on to feed the stories we've created that hold negative beliefs about others and ourselves.

Honey, I'm Home

Let's say your husband leaves for a round of golf saying he will be home no later that 5:00 p.m. It turns out that the golf course was backed up because of crowds. The golfers were held up at every hole. Your husband gets home much later than he said he would. He walks in and you say, "You obviously like spending time with your golf friends more than with me." That is an evaluation.

An observation of this event would go something like this. "Wow, you said you'd be home by 5:00 and it is 6:15." Then before getting mad you might ask a question to elicit more information such as "Why are you so much later than you said you would be?"

Accusing your husband of liking his golf friends more than he likes you comes from an *interpretation* of the event that is not based on what really happened. Rather, it comes from feelings of insecurity and the negative thought patterns that follow them. If you continue to interpret rather than observe the events that unfold around you, it will cause you to experience those same feelings of insecurity or fear, over and over again. Moreover, doing so will reinforce the negative thought patterning that follows those negative emotions, continually locking you into a cycle of misery.

When you become a *master observer,* you will put yourself on the threshold of unlimited possibilities in your life because you won't be locked in cycles of pain.

Imagine, if you thought you were stuck with your first car, your first home, or your first set of clothing. Say that the car, the home, and the clothes were all twenty to thirty years old by now. They're outdated, breaking down and falling apart, and not serving you well anymore. For some reason, you had the idea that you had to keep them *forever*, whether or not they were working for you. You've gotten so used to this old stuff you hardly notice, anymore, how difficult and challenging it makes your life. Then one day, your banker comes to you and says, "Hey, you have more money than you would ever need to buy a new car, new home, and new clothing. Let's take a look at what you have and see if you want to hang on to it, or if you want to use the money you have to get something new that works better." What a windfall! You're not stuck with old junk that doesn't work anymore. This is what observation does for you. It allows you to see what you're working with. You wake up and realize you're not stuck with these worn-out old thought patterns and negative emotions that are really *not* working for you anymore! Hallelujah! Amen! Life is good! From this point you can really move forward!

Third Observation Skill: Observe the Feelings in Your Body

Now, we move on to the third area of observation. This is the area in which we learn to *observe what is going on in our bodies.* In Chapter 5, "Emotions: Your Mind/Body Connection," we discussed how our entire bodies receive electrical and chemical signals from our thoughts. Our cells have neural receptors that receive messages constantly, from emotional chemicals that are continually triggered by both conscious and subconscious thoughts. Tuning into our entire body as we experience life and interact within our relationships... gives us genuine clues into our actual state of mind. This requires pausing for a moment and observing how we feel in our bodies, or how different parts of our bodies are feeling, especially when we are engaged in a stressful exchange.

Candice's Story

Candice was distraught about the way things were going at work. In her executive position, she had a lot of autonomy and a lot of authority. She was paid very well and could dictate her own hours. She liked her job. She liked her boss. So why was she feeling so out of sorts about going to work each day?

To get to the bottom of her difficulty, we had to consult the part of her mind that existed in her body. The mind itself was too linear and logical to get the job done. We put her in a light trance state, through hypnosis, and started to go through a day at work, subconsciously, noticing how the body felt as she went about her tasks.

We came to a point in her trance session, where she had to interface with a supervisor who was actually her peer. As she envisioned this particular supervisor once again adding to her already-weighty workload, she immediately felt sharp pains in her abdomen. She suddenly realized that what this person expected was completely out of line with the objectives and definition of her role in the company.

Before we had our session, out of a sense of duty, Candice had accepted job responsibilities that were in conflict with her real objectives; the ones she had been hired to accomplish. After our session, which allowed her to get in touch with her body/mind and observe the things she was feeling in her body, she admitted that she'd been getting these sharp abdominal pains at work, but hadn't made the connection to their source. They usually happened when she needed to have direct contact with this particular supervisor. Her body/mind had been communicating to her that there was a conflict that needed to be addressed, because the incongruence was making her sick.

When we finished the hypnotic session, Candice left feeling much lighter and knowing exactly what she needed to do to straighten out the situation at work and bring balance back to her role there. Once she got back to work and addressed the situation with the people involved, the former pains became conspicuously absent!

Learning to Use Your Body as a Barometer to Observe What's Happening

The body is a very accurate barometer of emotional and mental turmoil. If you learn to observe what is happening in your body, it will usually lead you to a greater understanding of a situation. The body also gives great feedback when you're on the right track. I encourage my clients to tune in to specific parts of their bodies and ask what is happening. What do they need to learn from this pain, discomfort, or even illness?

Years ago, I would have considered myself to be nuts for this kind of behavior. I mean asking your lower back why it locks up every time you need to deal with your controlling mother...? Come on! But you might be surprised by the story it will tell you. What I learned, once I got past my youthful ignorance, is that every cell of the body is a live, intelligent entity, and full of information. Why ignore such a great resource of information that would support your well-being and wellness?

It is extremely important to stay neutral when you tune into your body. Try not to judge what you're feeling, and most importantly, don't allow yourself to get into a fearful space and imagine that all kinds of bad things might be happening inside of you. Simply put a hand over the affected area, or at least imagine touching it in your mind. Breathe deeply, close your eyes if you can, and ask what this pain or illness means. Try not to project any thoughts or emotions into the process, just be still and listen. You will be amazed at what your body will let you know! Oftentimes, you will be able to get in touch with the very events or emotional states that allowed this pain or illness to manifest.

The art of observation is the second pillar in your life transformation. If you can remember to observe your thoughts as they form, to observe events as they unfold (rather than evaluating them), and also to observe the feelings in your body, you can free yourself from unnecessary conflict, pain, and turmoil that might otherwise go unchecked. Practicing observation daily, may make you suddenly feel like you've sprouted new wings that can take you in all kinds of new directions.

Chapter Eight
The Third Pillar: Choice

"Will you or won't you have it so?" is the most probing question we are ever asked; we are asked it every hour of the day, and about the largest as well as the smallest, the most theoretical as well as the most practical, things. We answer by consents or non-consents and not by words. What wonder that these dumb responses should seem our deepest organs of communication with the nature of things!"
—William James, The Principles of Psychology

As observers of our thoughts, we can decide if old perceptions and beliefs are working for us or against us. If we decide that the patterns of thought we hold are keeping us from getting what we truly want from our lives, then we are ready to activate the next crucial step of transformation, which is *choice*. This is the point in our growth where we begin to feel the unlimited possibilities of our existence. Owning our power to choose allows us to surrender old thoughts, beliefs, and self-righteous positions that have kept us from being all that we can be. When we deliberately release obsolete thought patterns and replace them with thoughts that bring harmony and success into our lives, we are giving permission to our most creative selves to come out of hiding.

Choice Allows Us to Write and Then Rewrite Our Stories

Our creator endows us with the sacred gift of free choice. It is our birthright. It truly is the most important and powerful tool we own as conscious creators of our own lives. We each may choose how and what to think, how to behave, and how and what we want to be.

Every choice we make in our lives, no matter how big or small, causes what eventually becomes the reality we live in. In each moment of our existence there is a choice. *Nothing* is set in stone about the way we think, feel, or behave.

What we think, how we feel about ourselves and others, and the way we behave, have all come about through thousands of little choices we have made along the way.

Your future is being created this moment by each choice you will make today, next week, and next month.

The stories we tell about our lives have developed from our own internal representations as we've processed our experiences, and the resulting *choices* we made as we processed those experiences.

The reason two people in the same situation can believe two completely different versions of something that happened, and how it affected them is that each *chose* to focus on a different angle of the situation. Say, two boys are in the car with their mother and the car stalls out, right on a train track with a train barreling toward them. A Good Samaritan sees the trouble and quickly helps the boys and mother to safety, just in the nick of time; right before the train hits the car and demolishes it. The first boy was completely focused on the stranger's kindness and feels tremendous relief and gratitude that his life was saved. The second boy was focused on the memory of the train speeding toward their car ready to crush them all, and the terrifying sound of crashing metal as it hits. He feels a fear and helplessness from the unexpected threat to all of their lives.

These two different focuses would undoubtedly influence each child and create lasting mental filters and belief systems. New experiences would continue to be processed through the lens of the dramatic event… affecting each boy's perceptions of subsequent events for years to come.

Children often don't have the awareness skills that would enable them to switch focus away from something negative to something positive. Whereas, adults *do* have the capability to choose what they focus on: the goodness of strangers versus the dangers of the world. As parents, we can guide our children and influence what *they* focus on by modeling positive thinking and gratitude.

You can see how awareness and a more deliberate strategy of choice can change the story of our lives so dramatically. Especially, considering there are *thousands* of choices we make each day that we're often not even aware of.

Letting Our Conscious Creator Choose Deliberately

When we want something to change in our lives, it is acutely important to learn to deliberately use this precious tool of choice to magnify the greatest qualities of our souls, and to begin to live in alignment with our true purpose.

Inside each of us at the level of our soul is a wiser, higher version of ourselves. This version of "self" is sometimes called our conscious creator, which is the same part of the "mind" that can observe the thoughts our brain is thinking. When I talk about the conscious creator, the observer, and the soul mind, I am referring to the same thing.

Don't Let Old Choices Get in the Way of Your Masterpiece

So how do we learn to utilize this tool of choice to make a real difference in our lives? We first must become cognizant of the present moment. In each moment we must think, speak, and take action with deliberate awareness. Instead of allowing our conditioned mind to run on autopilot, recycling repetitive, destructive thought patterns that keep us stuck in our sameness, we must let the conscious creator beyond the mind take the wheel. As soon as you start to practice deliberate choice through your conscious creator, you will feel a sense of freedom, space, and serenity. This is because a lot of what clutters our minds each day is useless debris, which serves *no* constructive purpose. Allowing unnecessary thoughts to litter our minds is like choosing them, again and again.

Imagine being a masterful painter trying to paint a beautiful canvas. Every time you settle in to create your masterpiece, a hurricane comes through throwing dirt and debris all over the canvas and creating a loud, distracting hum that makes it impossible for you to focus or continue painting. This hurricane turns your attention away from your creation and focuses it on fear and destruction. As unpleasant and frustrating as this scenario sounds, this is the mental condition most of us live in much of the time. The minute our conscious creator settles in to create something wonderful and new, our mental hurricane blows in cluttering our minds with useless debris, distracting us from our creative flow, and forcing our attention on fears, insecurities, and self-destructive thoughts.

It is impossible to get into a mode of conscious creativity when you are controlled by endless thought patterns. Negative mental patterns are responsible for the creation of the worst side of our ego-selves; a part that keeps projecting the past into the future. The ego chooses to keep the past alive because without the past, it knows it would die.

We often see this phenomenon in people with a mentality of victimhood. Their ego relies upon an endless stream of negative thoughts and belief patterns to keep recreating itself. It would cease to exist if the stories of being victimized in the past weren't being relived again and again. People become enslaved to a life of misery because they fail to understand their power of deliberate choice.

Natalie's Story

Natalie was a very successful young woman. She had finished her master's degree and was teaching biology at a prominent college. Throughout her educational experience she had achieved numerous awards for excellence. But in spite of her accomplishments in academia, Natalie was unhappy. She complained about the family problems she'd experienced with different family members throughout her life.

As she related her story to me in our first session, she discussed issues that she had cycled through with each of her relatives at different times. The common factor was that she was always the one at odds with someone. At that time, she was in the middle of a standoff with her mother. She felt that after her parent's divorce, when she was four, her mother hadn't been there enough for her. She also had a lot of negative feelings about her brothers and a couple of her sisters… saying they hadn't treated her right in her childhood and adolescence.

She had positive things to say about her father, although he had often been absent and distracted throughout her youth. He had addictions, which had led to some ugly behaviors that she had witnessed in her early years. It became apparent that what she seemed to like the most about her father, in spite of his apparent weaknesses, was that he always lavished praise upon her. He would tell her how brilliant she was and point out how much more she had accomplished than some of her other siblings. He told her she was the one out of all of them who could achieve high status in any profession she chose.

What began to stand out in our conversations was that Natalie's mother and siblings had a communication style that was more honest than her own. Their remarks were often blunt and to the point. They were upfront about issues they thought needed to be addressed, and didn't sugarcoat the points they felt needed to be made. As a result, some family interactions had become confrontational over the years.

It became evident to me that Natalie had hair-trigger defensiveness when someone didn't agree with her. She had no awareness of this herself. In most of the scenarios, she decried the maligning she had suffered at the hands of her cruel and insensitive siblings. In her mind, every negative thing she had experienced in her life was because of something one of her family members did to her, or did not do for her.

I could see, based on her own descriptions, that much of what had actually taken place through the years were normal sibling disagreements and entanglements that Natalie couldn't cope with because of a belief and value system that had been constructed in her own mind… a belief system which made it impossible for her to feel happiness. The belief system she subconsciously carried told her that she had to be perfect to be loved. She had created a false ego around that belief. This ego had constructed a very strict rule, which insisted on *everyone* acknowledging that *everything* she said and did was, in fact, perfect.

Her number one value in life was to be put on a pedestal. It became evident that this was her highest-ordered value because one by one, she had cut off many of the important relationships in her life, including those with her immediate family. Natalie had cast off family members if they had disagreed with her about one thing or another as families do. Always being right, and always being acknowledged as perfect had actually become more important to Natalie, than being a participant in loving relationships that had a normal measure of ups and downs and of give and take.

Unfortunately, Natalie moved on before we could finish our work together. Her complete refusal to honestly observe herself and to examine the choices that had led to her most destructive beliefs and values… made it impossible for her to move forward. Her deeply entrenched fear of being unlovable had created an ego-monster inside of her that desperately needed to be put on a pedestal in order to be happy. Although it had caused her tremendous pain, loneliness, and constant strife in relationships, her destructive ego-monster fought hard to stay alive. In the long run, it won again; causing her to avoid observing the truth inside and to *choose* differently.

Some very simple new choices, such as choosing to forgive loved ones for their imperfections, choosing to acknowledge *her* part in the family dynamics and interactions, and choosing to allow others to have their own beliefs or positions (over her need to be right) would have caused profound change in Natalie's life. Those simple choices would have created an important shift, in her ability to feel the joy she desperately wanted, within her important relationships. Choosing differently would have also freed her from the claws of a broken ego... allowing the most beautiful qualities of her soul to shine through.

When we over-identify with the mind, we believe we are our minds. An ego of any kind is a creation of the mind. That doesn't mean that every type of ego is necessarily destructive. All of us have an ego. It is a normal and necessary part of the human condition. It is when we allow the ego our mind has constructed, to take over our essential soul-self and make our most important choices that we end up in misery. One of the most important prayers/affirmations I use is to ask that my ego be in alignment with my soul.

Whenever I find myself becoming overly fearful and worried or unusually defensive and angry, I check in with my essential soul-self. I get honest with myself and observe the thoughts and feelings I am having. This habit helps me return to better choices that will allow me to experience peace, harmony, and success—rather than grief and turmoil. The transformational steps leading up to the choice step are extremely important. Life transformation requires humility to make authentic, lasting change.

You Always Own the Right to Choose Something Different

As you are reading this, you may be feeling that your life experiences were uniquely harsh; you have truly experienced more than your share of cruel or hateful behaviors from the people in your life, and it would be impossible to overcome them. You may be feeling that the lot you've been given is more than anyone can handle, and your negative feelings are justified. You may feel that choosing to let go and move on from traumatic events and negative feelings is not an option for you. I would beg to differ. Many real people have overcome seemingly insurmountable difficulties, and risen to become a grander version of who they were.

Nothing can hold the human spirit back in its determination to overcome hardship. Throughout the world, people conquer devastating loss, oppression, abuse, illness, grief, and neglect every single day. The way they rise above their desperate circumstances is by tapping into that unstoppable power within.

Each person, who has prevailed through indescribable hardship, has made a *conscious choice* to rise to something greater than his or her troubles, or those who may have contributed to them. Like them, no matter what scenarios you have experienced, so far, you still have the power *now* to choose your perception of those experiences. You have the power to put the past behind you and release it forever. This power comes to you through your own choice.

You also have the power to choose any thought you want, and if you choose positive, life-giving thoughts, each of those thoughts you choose will begin to reshape your life in a miraculous way. However, if you keep choosing the same thoughts, beliefs, and righteous positions, your life will stay exactly the same.

It's Not All about You

A common thread in the challenges that exist within relationships is the tendency for us to personalize the actions of others. This happens more commonly within our closest relationships, but it also occurs in professional relationships and in interactions between the most casual acquaintances, such as checkout clerks and store customers. Depending on our own level of emotional vulnerability, we can get slightly offended or thoroughly devastated by the behaviors or actions of others.

Those who personalize the behavior of others are also the most susceptible to sadness, defeat, depression, and low confidence. Someone says or does something, and the words or actions are interpreted as a personal attack against them... triggering defenses that they use to try to protect the vulnerability they feel inside.

A vulnerability that comes from their own imbedded programming, which says they aren't good enough or something is wrong with them. We all have little bits of this programming somewhere inside of us. This programming causes us to choose to make an undesirable action that someone just committed…all about us.

Here's the reality of relationships. When people say or do something hurtful or insensitive it is truly more about *them* than it is about you. I know from the many hours I've spent under the tutelage of Deepak Chopra, that one of truths he consistently repeats is that *everyone* is doing his or her best from his or her own state of consciousness. It is true that often people are rude, insensitive, unkind, impatient, and intolerant. But how freeing is it to know that their actions come from the level of consciousness they operate at, and not from any reality about you?

Deepak also teaches that when you are not affected by flattery or criticism; you are truly free. When we rely on the opinions or evaluations of others to build or destroy us, we are forever being rocked from side to side never finding our truth or our center. Choosing to be graciously detached from the appraisals, evaluations, and opinions of others will give you unprecedented power over your state of mind.

Each Day of Your Life the World Is Wide Open to Your Interpretation

Every choice you make in your life can mean the difference between experiencing lightness and joy, or experiencing deep sorrow. Consider the possibilities in the following choices.

- You can choose to carry a grudge forever, or you can choose to forgive.

- You can choose to focus each day on what's missing in your life, or you can choose to wake up each day and count your blessings.

- You can choose to keep finding someone to blame, for the way you feel or to take responsibility for your feelings.

- You can choose to criticize those around you and degrade them by continually finding fault, or you can choose to let the magic of your unconditional love create a space for them to grow.

- You can choose to focus on your imperfections each day, so that you never feel good enough, or you can choose to be comfortable in your own skin acknowledging your strengths and realizing there is no standard of perfection.

- You can choose to allow someone to cross personal boundaries and keep feeling resentful about it, or you can choose to truthfully and directly communicate your personal boundaries and honor them yourself.

- You can choose to stay in a mentally, physically, or emotionally abusive situation, or you can choose to find other options and leave.

- You can choose to continue believing that you are not good enough to achieve your greatest dreams, or you can choose a plan of action and start moving toward them.

- You can choose limits for yourself, or you can choose to break through previously imposed limits and raise the bar higher and climb over it.

- You can choose to live in fear of what might happen; thus, preventing yourself from taking decisive action, or you can choose to move forward and trust God and the universe to support you at all levels.

- You can choose to focus on events that provide reasons or excuses why you can't take action now, or you can choose to just start taking one step at a time to set the things you want in motion.

- You can choose to let the ever-changing, dynamic nature of life stop you in your tracks in a vain attempt to keep everything predictable, or you can choose to move with the flow of life's changes and find ways to adapt and grow.

- You can choose to keep re-telling the same old story, or you can end the old story and choose to begin to re-write a new story for your life.

- You can choose the destructive power of fear, or you can choose the life-giving power of love.

Choice Inventory Exercise

Each and every moment of your life provides an opportunity for choice. The exercise below is designed to build awareness of the power of choice into your life each day. It is designed to help you tune in to this ever-present choice-making process, and to start to use that process more deliberately to create greatness in your life. This process takes place at the end of the day when you are looking at it, retrospectively.

Ask, "What thoughts am I choosing, right now?" Then write down the seven most prevailing thoughts you've had today, regardless of what they were or how many times you thought them. Deliberate thinking says: if you're having them—you're choosing them.

1. _____

2. _____

3. _____

4. _____

5. _____

6. _____

7. _____

Write down seven key actions you chose to take today, even if they were simple things like having a conversation or taking a nap. Not choosing is the same as choosing. If you chose not to do something that you needed or wanted to do write down the reason.

1. _____

2. _____

3. _____

4. _____

5. _____

6. _____

7. _____

Now, I'd like you to think about the power of those choices. Go back to your two lists, and next to each thought choice and each action choice, write the words "positive," "negative," or "neutral."

A positive choice means the thought or action supports a higher vision of your life including relationships, health, career, and so on.

A negative choice means the thought or action degrades the highest vision of your life in any area.

A neutral choice can be fine: that you are just maintaining your life, which is necessary. But it can also mean you are just settling for maintaining status quo, just getting by, or accepting less than all that you want. Examining the choices you make, each day, can become a great personal revelation in your life transformation.

In this very moment and in the next, what thought, idea, or action could you choose that would start to shift you to a higher level of living and being? Will you claim the power this very moment holds for you and choose to deliberately create something new through your choices? Or will you continue on autopilot letting the old programs guide you numbly to the same places you've been so many times before?

If you are ready to commit to lasting change in your life through the powerful transformational pillar of choice, then the next seven choice commitments are about claiming your power of choice *now*.

Write down seven distinctly different, new, and improved choices of thought or of action that you will begin to implement starting now.

1. _____

2. _____

3. _____

4. _____

5. _____

6. _____

7. _____

Discovering and Choosing the Personal Philosophy of Someone Who Has What You Want

Choice makes one human being different from another. What we've chosen to focus on and what we've chosen to do, as a result of that focus, is what has made each of us who we are. Our choices have shaped the lives we are living.

A really wonderful coaching tool that I teach is the principle of emulating someone who is already doing or being successful, at what you want to do or be. For instance, if you have always wanted to be fit and slender find out what people who are fit and slender do. What are their eating, sleeping, and exercising habits? What is their personal philosophy? Find out and *start choosing to do some or all of the same things.*

If you want to become a successful salesperson talk to as many successful salespeople as you can, and find out their personal philosophy. How many hours do they work? What are the best prospecting hours? What marketing techniques have they found to be the best use of their time? What have they discovered is a waste of time? Get all of the information you can, and then *make the choices for yourself* that you know are already working, for those who are successful in the way *you* want to be successful.

Choosing to be around the people you *want* to be like greatly accelerates change in your life. Look around you. Notice your peer group. Take into account all of the things about them that characterize their identities. Does the group of people that you spend your time with embody the character qualities and lifestyle you aspire to?

You don't necessarily have to recreate the wheel when you desire massive life change and self-growth. There is a reason we don't live on a planet all by ourselves. Human beings require the interaction, feedback, and support of one another. Connection to people is one of the essential human needs.

As you go through this discovery process write down what you learn. Keeping notes will help you make a concrete plan of action and put you in a different state of consciousness. The more you immerse yourself in the consciousness of success and happiness, even if it starts out as someone else's happiness, the happier and more successful your consciousness will become.

The Most Powerful "Choice" Question

The greatest influence we can have over our lives is through our choices. Harmony and success can only come into your life through the power of choice. Throughout your day pause often and ask yourself, "Am I deliberately choosing that which leads to my greatest self… living my greatest life?" On a daily basis, honor this powerful and precious gift of the Divine: the gift of free choice.

What will you choose in the next moment, the next day, and the next week of your life? Choice is the third pillar of transformation.

Chapter Nine

The Fourth Pillar: Responsibility

"Responsibility is the price of greatness."
—Winston Churchill

⚜

The fourth pillar, responsibility, is like a pillar made of stone. It is a foundational element of transformation. It connects you to all the virtues within that are essential to your grandest success and thereby allows you to be the architect of your life.

Think back to the first time in your life that you remember taking responsibility for something that happened or needed to happen. It might have been the first time your mom said you could walk home from school by yourself. Maybe it was the first time you got on a bus and rode in a vehicle not driven by your parents. It could have been when one of your parents told you to keep an eye on a younger brother or sister. If you can get in touch with one of these memories, then try to tap into the feeling of being responsible for something for the first time... of owning the outcome of something that mattered.

Move forward a little bit *now* on your timeline. As you grew and matured you undoubtedly took on bigger responsibilities. Thinking back, again, remember the first time you had to take over and be *fully* in charge of something. Maybe it was the first time you completed a research project by yourself. Perhaps it was when you babysat for several kids and took care of all of their needs on your own. It might have been when you stepped in, when nobody else would, to stop a fight. Whatever that memory is for you, when you go back to it get in touch with the feeling of complete ownership of what you were doing, and the personal power and satisfaction you felt from having responsibility.

If we can recall those first feelings we felt when we willingly accepted responsibility for something that mattered, we usually associate a sense of freedom and independence with the experience. The sense of satisfaction we felt on the occasion of such experiences came from the authority we felt over our own lives, as we recognized our dominion over them. The more we were allowed to test our skills of discernment and the more we accounted for the choices we made from that discernment, the stronger our sense of responsibility and ownership became.

No One Owes You a Living—Except You

It seems that responsibility is not popular in some arenas of today's pop culture. All you have to do is to occasionally tune in to your television, to witness another Hollywood diva citing her latest disclaimer about her role in what is happening in her own life. These people appear to be stunned by the natural consequences of their behavior, as if they had no part in creating the outcome of their choices.

Another responsibility-challenged segment in American society today is a portion of the homeless population that includes young, healthy, usually male individuals who have simply decided they don't want to be responsible for their own food and shelter. I live in a large metropolitan area where a couple of years ago, this particular group of people had invaded the quaint streets surrounding our major university. Now, it may not seem like much of a problem to have young people hanging out each day, where many other young people are residing while they get their education. The reason it became a huge problem here was that *these* homeless people didn't politely hold out their hands and ask for help. Rather, they asked for money and then got angry and belligerent if they were refused a handout. Perhaps you've experienced something similar in your own city?

The attitude these people adopted is one of shifting responsibility for themselves and their survival onto perfect strangers. It is not surprising that they behaved the way they did, when their demands were not met. Someone who is completely irresponsible in his or her own life is much more prone to hostility, resentment, and fear. Negative emotions that are felt from a refusal to accept responsibility leave a person feeling out of control.

All types of people who operate in irresponsible ways (not just celebrities and homeless people) have somehow ended up with the mental programming that says:

- "Responsibility weighs me down."

- "Responsibility robs me of my freedom."

- "Responsibility prevents me from doing what I want to do."

Such beliefs are fallacies. Practicing discipline and accountability to yourself actually opens every door imaginable to you, because now everything is in your hands. Taking hold of the wheel of your own life allows *you* to drive yourself any distance in any direction you want to go.

Who's Driving Your Bus?

Imagine that you get on a bus and you aren't quite sure where you should be going, but instead of reading the map to learn of all of the possible places you could go, plotting an exciting journey, and then getting behind the wheel yourself to make sure you get there; you give up and let someone else figure out where you should go and how you should get there. You then let them take over the wheel and drive.

How would it feel to have not had any say in this journey that could have been so remarkable had you planned it? How deep might your regret be, when you realize this person you allowed to chauffeur you on this important journey doesn't really even understand *what* places are important for you to get to, or *how* to get to your dream destination. The driver's sense of direction happens to be very poor when it comes to navigating this journey for you, and he or she was a little indifferent to begin with. The driver is only driving this bus because you allowed it, and not because the driver is passionate about the journey.

As you move along on this journey with someone else at the wheel, you realize you are being taken down rough roads. Your driver is bouncing you through potholes and dangerously swerving to dodge obstacles that appear in front of the bus. You are being thrown and bumped around, without the vantage point you might have if you had chosen to drive. At times, you feel restless and without a purpose. It actually feels boring and unfulfilling to stand by, unengaged, not contributing to the success of this journey that could have been so amazing. Other times, you feel tremendously scared and anxious, as if you have no control over your life. This feeling of fear isn't surprising. After all, when you let someone or something outside of you drive your life, you really don't have much influence over the outcome. You are not controlling your destiny.

Now, imagine if you sat down again with this same wonderful opportunity in front of you—a journey anywhere in your very own motor coach! This time you get to plan the destination, the route you will be taking, and how long you want to spend getting from here to there. You plan carefully, checking out the best routes and using your best strategy to avoid bad roads and pitfalls along the way. You feel confident in this journey because *you* will be at the wheel. If challenges come up you will be in front to deal with them, not standing helplessly in the back feeling the worst of the bangs and bumps.

This bus journey is your life. Which way will you choose to take it? Will you shirk responsibility and allow yourself to be a helpless passenger, by riding in the back of the bus, and allowing any number of unnamed people or events to drive you places you did not choose? Or will you seize the opportunity to plot your own adventure; one that allows you to be in charge, to experience great things, and also to experience the tough things that will teach you to be great. The journey that you are responsible for is the one that helps to uncover the best parts of yourself, and the ultimate purpose of your life.

Who drives your bus? Sometimes it's an abusive parent, or a former lover, or ex-spouse on whom we would like to blame our current state. Your bus driver may not even be a person. It could be an illness, injury, or bad experience that you finally succumbed to and allowed to take over your identity. Oftentimes, we go through a scary illness or bad experience, and from that day forward we let that experience drive and direct every moment of the rest of our lives. Whomever or whatever we continue to hold up as the reason that we can't do what we want or need to do... is the thing that we allow to drive us.

Life is designed to challenge us. The challenges and adversity are there to allow us opportunities to learn and grow. Letting challenges defeat us and take over our lives is like saying, "I give up. You win you nasty little challenge." Instead of recognizing the opportunity to become stronger and better and to evolve; sometimes, we retreat and say to the bad event or person, "You really got me down this time so I guess I'll just step back and let you own me, forever."

Don't ever, ever back away from your life... especially when you're going through a challenge. Remember that this is your golden opportunity to grow, to change, to become the best you!

After challenging life events, it is especially important to make a deliberate choice to take back your life. Regardless of what you've suffered, making the decision to take back the responsibility for your life, will make it possible for you to continue to rise above and transcend *any* adversity that comes your way. Adversity and challenge represent *great* growth opportunities.

If each day, you decide to take responsibility for your life, nothing can ever take over your life and consume you. You will continue to be in charge and to be powerful, and to push forward in the direction you want to go.

Responsibility Brings Out the Genius in You

How many times in our lives have we found ourselves making excuses or blaming someone else for something that did or didn't happen; something that would have made our lives better in some way? Whenever we convince ourselves that someone outside of us is in charge of the outcome of our lives, we immediately feel out of control. Taking full responsibility for everything that happens in our lives allows us to feel powerful and in control. When we stop blaming others and making excuses, most of the problems in our lives begin to miraculously resolve themselves.

Accepting responsibility for what happens in our lives and for what we want, instantly causes our minds to shift focus. A mental shift propels us to find solutions and create plans that move us forward in the direction we want to go. As you learned in previous chapters, the mind is infinitely powerful and resourceful. When we blame others and make excuses, we shut ourselves off from our own resourcefulness—our own genius.

Thoughts of blame and excuse-making create an operating pattern that says, "I'm not capable of resolving this issue or finding solutions. It is someone else's job to fix it for me." Responsibility-shifting thought patterns could instantly cut you off from your own creativity and ability to make things happen in your life. You will begin to feel the power of *ownership* over your life if, on the other hand, you are willing to take whatever situation life hands you and say:

- "I will find a solution to this problem."

- "I will get to the bottom of this issue and start to move forward again."

- "I will tap into my inner strength and ingenuity, and be open to any and all resources that support me in getting through this."

- "I will lead the way in my own life, not follow."

- "I will trust in the infinite, divine power of God, and the universe to support me in every step of my journey."

What Makes People Hang Their Responsibility on Someone Else?

Why do so many people have difficulty accepting responsibility for their lives? People, who shift blame and responsibility, somehow feel that doing so will exonerate them from the outcome of their lives. It is really a form of self-deception because no one owns the outcome of your life except you—period. Taking full responsibility requires guts and decisive action, and this can sometimes be a bit taxing and strenuous.

Some folks think it is easier just to give up and shift responsibility for their lives to someone or something other than themselves. If this seems tempting to you, remember that while it might seem easier at the moment, doing so will only set you up for a life that feels completely out of control. I don't know *anyone* who feels peace, happiness, and success when his or her life feels out of his or her *own* control. Whatever gut-wrenching, determined action it takes… taking back your life and all of the responsibility for it is the *only* way to experience true harmony, happiness, and success.

Relinquishing responsibility in any area of your life, to any degree, essentially means letting someone else decide your life experiences for you. It means giving up the power and authority over your life that is meant for you alone—as a sacred gift from your Creator. God gave ownership of your life on Earth to one person: you. The key to claiming this ownership is learning to rely more on your internal resources, than on any other external resource. You are the only one equipped (through your own heart and your own mind) to tap into your desires, talents, and creativity. If you keep looking outside to find meaning, purpose, and fulfillment your search will come up empty. You are the only author qualified to write the great story of your life.

The Ever-changing Nature of Life

I find that one of the things that most intimidates people from accepting responsibility is the ever-changing nature of life itself. There is something within each of us that tends to crave certainty. We all have a need to know that we can count on being safe, loved, and provided for. These needs are basic, primitive, and universal. For some, the need for certainty is stronger than it is for others, but within all of our physiology, the most primitive part of our brain structure is set up to send up little red flags if something changes on the horizon. This inherent brain design is perfect for keeping us safe, and it was especially helpful in ancient times; since noticing an impending change in weather, or the menacing sound of a predatory animal, determined our survival on the planet.

Life has advanced, but the primitive brain structure is still there. As consciousness evolves, people are getting more opportunities to evolve and become better. Evolution involves change. Certainty is somewhat of an illusion, as the only thing that is truly certain in this world we live in is *change*. Some people cringe when they hear this. The need for certainty in some is *so* great that they will do just about anything to keep things predictable, and often this includes turning responsibility for their lives over to someone else. Even if the predictable is a miserable existence, they at least know what to expect.

One of the essential qualities of life is its ever-changing nature. It is within the realm of movement and change that unlimited possibilities exist to learn, grow, and create something new or different. Nothing moves in stagnant water. Without movement, everything sits and putrefies or deteriorates. When you understand that the true nature of life is like a ceaselessly flowing river, you begin to get comfortable in allowing the river to move you along. Many opportunities and options will flow to you, and it will be your responsibility to decide to take them or wait for something else. There will also be things flowing to you that are difficult or will challenge you. Again, it is your opportunity and responsibility to decide if those things will block your movement, or if you will you embrace them and use them to make you stronger—thereby accelerating your forward journey toward better things. Each time you embrace change and movement and take full responsibility for its presence in your life, your level of consciousness and learning will be elevated.

I recommend using a little prayer or intention each day that goes something like this:

Infinite God, let me embrace each opportunity this day holds for me to grow and learn. Let me recognize the infinite possibilities in the ever-changing world I live in. May I be awake to the possibilities; to the wonderful surprises that await me! May I be alive in the movement, and dance with the music of life that surrounds me! I release all fear of change, and lovingly embrace all of the wonderful changes, and new beginnings life has in store for me!

The Responsibility of Boundaries

Often, the clients with whom I work will lay responsibility for their happiness or their success on the behavior of someone close to them. They say things like, "I can't be happy in my relationship because he is always doing mean, inconsiderate things to me;" or "My job is terrible because she makes it impossible to resolve problems and work cooperatively." Disagreements and entanglements are a part of the reality of human relationships. One of the most effective and powerful ways to deal with these entanglements is by establishing personal boundaries, and then not allowing others to cross those boundaries.

Here is a step-by-step method for setting up healthy boundaries.

Decide on some specific, reasonable, healthy boundaries and write them down. For instance a boundary could be, "I will not stand there and let my partner berate me;" or "I will not argue facts with my co-worker without real evidence in front of us."

Decide on a specific action you will take if a boundary is crossed and write it down. This could be something as simple as saying to your partner, "I'm sorry, it is never okay to speak to me this way. If you would like to have a reasonable discussion, please let me know when you can speak calmly and respectfully." Then turn immediately and walk away. Do not go after the person or pursue his or her attention in any way. Letting the person make the decision to come back to you, to resolve the issue and start an honest, clear discussion, means he or she has already acknowledged and honored the boundary you set.

In the case of the co-worker, your statement might be something like, "I'm sorry, there is nothing productive about us wasting valuable time arguing. When one or both of us can get some supporting evidence to back up our assessment of the situation, then we can reconvene and make some real progress in resolving this." Once again, exit the situation with a calm, professional demeanor. Make sure the co-worker knows, for future reference, that you aren't willing to get sucked into petty arguments because they are not conducive to anyone's success.

Boundary-setting puts you in charge of the kind of personal interactions you are willing to be involved in. It releases blame that you might have tried to put on someone else, and that puts you in charge of your life.

Your Personal Commitment to Responsibility

The following is a short exercise to help put you in a deliberate state of responsibility consciousness. Below make a list of areas you can honestly say you have attempted, at one time or another, to shift responsibility away from yourself and to blame your state or situation on someone else. This list is a declaration of the areas in your life you are now willing to step up to and own, again, or perhaps own for the first time.

1. _____

2. _____

3. _____

4. _____

5. _____

6. _____

7. _____

When you actually make that decision to take control of your life and put yourself in the driver's seat, your life can become dynamic, rich, and passionate. Life is meant to be experienced, felt, and *lived*! Don't lose this gift by giving away ownership of yourself and your life. We simply cannot experience passion and joy for a life we refuse to fully own. Fully being in our lives, and fully owning the experiences that are created within them… creates exuberance and a zest for living that could never be felt by disconnecting.

Taking responsibility fosters some of your greatest virtues such as humility, courage, and creativity. This will result in the greatest *you* creating your greatest life.

Chapter Ten
The Fifth Pillar: Imagination

"I believe in the imagination. What I cannot see is infinitely more important than what I can see."
—Duane Michals

Now we move forward to the fifth pillar of transformation. Once we've come this far, it is time for the fun to begin! When you learn to actively use the transformational pillar of imagination, you will notice the walls of limitation begin quickly to crumble, expanding your world in all directions.

Every single thing that you have been, or that you will ever become, began in your imagination. The person you were, when you lacked the confidence to stand up and give a speech was originally created in your mind. You probably imagined yourself messing up or looking stupid, if you were to stand up in front of people to talk. When you were a teenager, if you were the person who always got dumped by a boyfriend or girlfriend, chances are that those break-ups started being played out in your imagination before they ever happened; possibly triggered by an insecurity about not being good enough.

If you were the star of the swim team, basketball team, or the lead in your school play, most likely you were able to picture yourself in those roles before they ever came to be. Whether you were the winner or loser, the honor roll student or the class clown, the leader of the group or the one who carries out the duties, all of the identities you've ever worn began in your imagination.

When you decide to reach a little higher, to achieve a greater level of success or to step into a role that is new and challenging, it is exceedingly important to have clear visions and feelings about the things you are aspiring toward. Your success or failure in every role you ever play will be played out in your imagination, before it plays out in the events of your life. Imagination is the arena within your mind where the colors, flavors, and qualities of experience are gathered and arranged, before they become woven into our lives. Most of us aren't aware that the results of the situations we find ourselves in are largely predetermined by our mental projections.

Ah, the Joy of Childhood Imagination

As children, our imaginations are in full bloom. We spontaneously choose to play out identities, roles, and scenarios that make us feel alive and wonderful. During the uninhibited, uncensored years of our youth, we allow ourselves (through the freedom of imaginative play) to become fully immersed in roles and identities... feeling the joy, the drama, and the victories of the archetypes we wish to become.

Children often spend many hours of playtime acting out the roles that sing to their hearts. Some little boys pretend to be a superhero or rescuer, confidently intervening in emergency situations... showing up with super strength to save the day. Others play at being the world's greatest basketball player or racecar driver. Everyone has seen a little girl glow, as she knows how dazzling she would be as a beautiful princess or a famous singer. Others play at being a mommy, doctor, or veterinarian knowing exactly how to comfort and care for anyone in need. Children also allow themselves the imaginative freedom to become horses, puppies, tigers, gorillas, or any other animal that seems to embody the qualities that they love.

Recapturing the Unbounded Imagination

As kids, we have no boundaries to what we believe we could become because we haven't gotten enough negative feedback, at that stage in our lives, to shut us off from any of our dreams. Well-meaning adults warning us of the difficulties and pitfalls that lay ahead of us haven't programmed our minds, yet. Therefore, our imaginations create infinite possibilities for us. At that point, we haven't been criticized or put down for not being realistic. We simply haven't experienced enough defeat or ridicule, to feel shame in thinking that we could actually have or be anything our hearts could desire.

By the time we reach our late teen years, we have usually had enough negative programming (through our experiences and interactions) that seeds of doubt in ourselves and our abilities begin to grow. In an effort to be socially accepted, teens often begin to play it safe or small in order to fit in. They will often minimize their talent or potential because of the risk of rejection or criticism from peers, and even well meaning parents. Parents, with no faith in their own ability to create a life of their dreams, might feel they are doing a disservice to their child, by encouraging them to think beyond the limitations they *themselves* feel. They believe they may be setting the child up for disappointment or failure by endorsing something they aren't sure of. Better to play it safe and be realistic... encouraging their children to do only what feels secure and predictable to *them*.

Many of us grow from children who imagine we can be or do anything, *into* adults who doubt our potential and feel we must limit ourselves to what we know is certain. As children, we allow ourselves to play the roles that spring from the untapped well within our hearts. As adults, we shut ourselves off from our hearts' desires, and often manage our lives through a safety net of logic and reason. Unfortunately, the subconscious programs instructing us on how to set up the blueprint for our lives are often laced with defeatism, negativity, and fear.

The imbedded mental programs many of us rely upon, to guide our lives, are the ones that keep reminding us of all of the ways we could fail. Since all of our beliefs and subsequent actions follow the thought programming operating our minds, it is not sensible to think that we can achieve success and happiness, by giving in to the negative thoughts that carefully push us away from our greatest potentials. It does not ultimately serve us to squelch our plans for greatness because the mind is subliminally sending out a signal of fear, which we've come to believe protects us from the great unknown.

Trusting Your Heart to Guide Your Imagination

Antoine de Saint-Exupéry said, "It is only with the heart that one can see rightly; what is essential is invisible to the eye." Learning to use your imagination requires tuning into the whisperings of the heart. This may take time and deliberate effort for some of us because many of us have shut ourselves off from the urgings of our heart, so often, that the heart has become very quiet. There is no need to fret that the urgings are gone forever, though. The minute we decide to open up to those messages of the heart, the louder and more present they become, and the stronger they resonate with our own unique purpose. Listening to the heart unblocks the imagination because we begin to feel the possibilities our life holds, at all levels of our being.

Our minds allow us to analyze, organize, and focus, but our hearts give us the clearest and purest direction to our greatest purpose. The heart, alone, cradles the deep wellspring of talents and gifts that are embedded in our souls. When we listen to the heart, we reconnect to our creator and the purpose of our being. Our hearts are the satellite links to our home… to all we are… and all that we are to become.

Like an overzealous security guard, the mind often reacts to the bold desires of the heart, trying to protect us from unknown possibilities and unchartered waters. But the heart speaks to us through our desires. The deepest yearnings of our hearts urge us toward that ultimate life, which creation holds for us. Inside we all want to be extraordinary in some way. We all want to have good things and do great things. We all want a life that matters.

Inside every heart is a sound, like a faraway train whistle that is calling us to our greatest adventure. When the mind scolds us and reminds us of our limitations, the heart is there with the courage to release the illusion of inadequacy encouraging us to sacrifice and to persevere. Whenever we've transcended hardship and risen to a better life, or decided to do something bigger and bolder than we'd ever done before, or triumphed over a challenge that seemed insurmountable, our heart's desire led the way.

The heart is the part of us that connects us to our guiding spiritual source. There is a special song the Creator wrote just for us. We can't truly *live* without opening ourselves and listening to the music inside, which comes to us from the heart and feeds our imagination.

Sadly, most people never truly learn to use their imaginations because it requires them to *trust* what their hearts are telling them. There is boldness to dreaming dreams that seem far beyond reach. Often, people come to see me with a deep, unnamed sense of dissatisfaction in their lives. For far too long, they have settled for less than what they were made to do. The story they have created around their dissatisfaction, often lets them pretend to be incapable of stepping outside of their own self-imposed box. They seek my help because they can't take the life they are living, anymore. It is if they are living as imposters in their own lives.

It takes the desire of the heart first, to direct the imaginative mind and dare it to dream and create; to be and become. Mastering the imaginative functions of the mind will be your most creative resource in the transformation of your life. Your own imagination will allow your life to continue to transform an infinite number of times, unbounded, and in every area of your existence.

How Do You Put Your Imagination to Work?

What does it mean to really use the imaginative mind? How do you really put your imagination to use in order to begin to actuate your dreams? Engaging the imagination (for the purpose of your greatest creation) goes far beyond setting a goal or making a list of what you want for your life. It is about using your mind to project yourself into any situation or role that you want to have in your life, in the future. It means allowing every sensory medium to take a journey through your mind to help you feel, see, taste, and smell anything you want before you actually have it.

One of the reasons that hypnotherapy is such a powerful tool for life-change is that we use a tremendous amount of guided imagery in a session. When I'm working with a client, after we've gone through some coaching and emotional clearing sessions, we then decide together exactly what experience the client wants in his or her life. I start by inducing the client into a relaxed state, so that the brain wave slows down and the subconscious mind becomes more available. I then guide him or her on a journey of the mind using all of the images, feelings, and sensations that make up the fabric of what it is that my client wants to experience.

Through experiments with scanning technology, science has proven that when we use the imagination, the brain registers and records the experience of our sensory imagery *exactly* in the same way and in the same areas of the brain that it would… if the experience were actually taking place in the physical world.

We've all had dreams from which we awaken with our hearts pounding in fear or our bodies humming in elation or joy. Sometimes, the dream experience is so real it causes us to cry out or awaken with tears streaming down our faces. It is often difficult, within our first moments of waking to determine that what we just experienced was a dream and not "real life" as we think of it. The sensations our brain and nervous system just registered in the dream state were activated *exactly* as if we had seen, felt, tasted, or smelled the elements in the dream experience.

When you simply imagine biting into a lemon, it activates the brain and registers the experience of a juicy, tart, wet sensation causing your tongue and lips to react in the same way they would have if you had really bitten into a lemon. The events occurring in the brain (from the imagined experience) are just the same as they would be if you had *actually* bitten into the lemon. All of the same chemicals are secreted, and the cascading physiological responses of the body follow.

The power of the imagination is why hypnotherapy and guided imagery (done on a repetitive basis) can help you create a new reality in your life. The more your brain experiences the sensations of a particular experience or way of being, the more it directs the chemistry of the entire mind/body to support that identity or experience. The entire imaginative experience becomes embedded in the cellular memory of the mind and body. It becomes *real*. It becomes who you are.

You may think you need a practitioner of hypnotherapy to accomplish what you want in your life. It certainly is helpful to have that kind of support, but you *don't need* to have someone else involved. You can learn to engage your imagination by using imagery on your own. As a child, this process came easily to you. While you might be a little rusty, right now, on the imagination front once you open up to it again, I promise that it won't take long before it becomes your best creative friend.

Imagining the Real into Life

The following imagery exercise will help you experience what you want, before it actually manifests in the physical form of your life. This exercise can be used for something as small as wanting to feel comfortable reaching out to make new friendships, or when you want a major life change that you've never experienced before, such as a new career or marriage. Practice the scene visualization each day until you begin to feel comfortable with the vision.

Decide on a new scenario that you would like to have playing out in your life *now*. It can be a new paradigm in career, relationships, service, or even an adventure that you are dreaming of having. Write down by hand (rather than on a computer) all of the details that describe and characterize this scenario you desire. The more detailed you are the better. If the change you desire is a broad lifestyle change, depending on the amount of time you have, you may want to break it into several smaller scenes and do a visualization of a different one each day. For example, if you want to be married and haven't met the right person, yet, you could have an entire scene about being at the right place at the right time and meeting someone. Instantly, you see and feel your eyes locking and lingering. You might then see both of you engaging in conversation, eagerly and naturally. When it is time to go you envision both of you being hesitant to leave each knowing there is so much more to say... and so on.

The next scene in your visualization could be after you've dated awhile and become very comfortable with one another. See and feel how both of you want to spend most of your time together. Then one day, you see each other pledging to spend your lives together. The scene or scenes after that could include planning a wedding, enjoying a fabulous honeymoon, and moving into your first home together.

Whether the scene or scenes of your imagery exercise involve small changes or big lifestyle changes, make sure that you imagine that it is happening right now in the present moment, and include:

- What you are seeing

- What you are hearing

- What you are smelling

- What you are tasting

- What you are feeling in terms of bodily sensations

- What you are feeling emotionally (for example, free, secure, loved).

- What your environment is like

- What your daily schedule is like

- The most important players with whom you are interacting

- Who your primary relationships are with

- The relational dynamic within those relationships

- Your creative role within this scenario

- How the future continues to unfold beyond the scenario

Once you have drafted a highly detailed description of the scene or scenes that you are envisioning… read through it several times, until you really get a good feeling for what it encompasses. Then sit back, close your eyes, and imagine that you have walked into a movie theater, and you are about to watch a movie on a screen about this life scenario you just invented and wrote down.

From your seat in the theater allow your planned movie scene to play out in your mind in a detailed manner including the colors, flavors, smells, tastes, feelings, and emotions you invented. Watch them unfolding like a rich motion picture on the screen, and watch yourself up there playing the role of the main character.

Enjoy the experience to the best of your ability. The more positive emotions you feel when you are engaging your imagination, the more neural connections your mind and body will make to support you having what you want.

After you've played the movie through once in your mind, imagine that you are walking up to the big screen, opening a door right in the center of it, and stepping into the movie. Allow yourself to play the movie once more. This time you are acting out your part from the inside rather than observing as a third entity. Feel the sensations, see the sights, smell the aromas, hear the sounds, let your tongue taste delicious things. Being inside your own life scenario movie adds another dimension of sensory reality to the experience you are planning to actually have happen in your life.

When you are finished playing the movie in your mind, and being in the movie, imagine the scene or scenes together in one still frame.

Next, imagine that you can shrink the huge screen down into one small, tasty cracker. See the entire image; all of the sensory images your film contains being reduced and concentrated into a bite-sized morsel. Imagine that this cracker contains the perfect codes to activate all of the changes you need, that would bring to life the scenario or life situation you desire. Then imagine yourself popping the cracker into your mouth, chewing it up, enjoying the tasty, crunchy sensation, swallowing it, and having all of the perfect encoding and patterns be absorbed into your body to become a part of you.

Don't be concerned if a voice ever pops up in your mind saying, "No way, this isn't real." Simply observe the negative thought like it is a fish swimming by. You see it, but then it's gone. Know that those types of thoughts come from old, negative programming, and that the more you repeat the visualizations of your life as you want it; the more your new, positive programming will override the old stuff.

It normally takes at least 30 days of consistent repetition to change mental programs and implement new programs. This exercise is *remarkably effective.* It engages the imaginative mind on multiple sensory levels. The feelings and thoughts that are engaged through this process cause things to *happen* within the body. Just as unharnessed, automatic, negative thinking changes body chemistry, your well-directed, positive thinking (about the life you want to create) is going to flood your bloodstream with chemicals that behave positively within your body/mind. The happy, positive chemicals will encode the feelings and experience into the permanent memory within the cells of your brain and body; thus, supporting the ultimate creation of the life experience that you desire and have spent time imagining.

Imagination in Action in Pop Culture

A good example of the power of the imagination is the phenomenon that takes place on the blockbuster TV show "American Idol." People from all walks of life come to an audition with the dream of going from their simple lives of obscurity to blockbuster stardom. They show up week after week reaching for their next personal level of excellence. They put themselves on the line, subjecting themselves to criticism of the judges and the evaluation of an audience of millions of TV viewers.

Personally, I am addicted to this show. What brings me back each week is the experience of witnessing the undaunted power of the human spirit at its best. The drama of seeing another human being put his or her vulnerability on the line by standing up and belting out another soul-baring performance, right after they were publicly slammed on their hindquarters by the infamous Simon Cowell, the week before (or sometimes minutes before) inspires me.

Before they ever arrive for their first audition, how many times must they have imagined themselves as America's newest star? Would there be any other way to be able to sustain their determination through such pressure and scrutiny? Like a modern-day revolt against the acceptance of anything less than all you want to be; these everyday revolutionaries, who perform each week, give me a reverence for the ability of the imaginative mind to create and recreate an identity from the raw desires of the heart.

Just to participate in the audition process before the fun even begins, the contestants stand in line, for days at a time, sleeping and eating on the piece of ground they happen to be standing on—in hopes of getting the chance to spend a few moments in front of three tired, jaded judges whom they are hoping will glimpse the star inside the auditioning singer... waiting to be set free.

There are even those like the lovable William Hung who became a huge hit in the first season. They have a pure spirit of hope and imagination, but no actual talent, and yet they manage to capture the hearts of America. We cheer for these people because of the contagious attraction that draws us to someone who feels the freedom to genuinely embrace the desires of his or her heart (and believe in them), regardless of what anyone else may think.

On Imagination

What an extraordinary thing the imagination is. The advent of every invention or piece of technology we enjoy today started in the imagination of someone like you; someone who noticed the need for something better, new, or different, and allowed his or her mind to reach into the unknown. Imagination lets us take the unknown and make it known to all who are waiting for solutions to their needs and wants. It is a pathway to bring something that is not yet realized into reality. Ask yourself what the world would be deprived of if men and women like Bill Gates, Martin Luther King, or Jean Nidetch (founder of Weight Watchers) hadn't embraced their guiding visions.

Bill Gates' dream was for every household and business to have a computer. Microsoft was born from his determination to create a user-friendly programming language. His dream has had a huge influence on our world. Jean Nidetch had a completely different vision back in the '60s, for the thousands of women who wanted to lose weight but found success at it difficult. She imagined that if she were able to gather women together, weekly, to support one another in reaching their weight-loss goals, they would achieve those goals more quickly and easily. Today millions of men and women around the world use the Weight Watchers' products and support services.

Not much more can be said about the vision of Martin Luther King, Jr. Within his imagination he held a new vision for the world that others were afraid to share. His willingness to share his vision of equality, courageously, caused a huge shift in the consciousness of the United States, and went onward to influence the entire worldview about the rights of all men and women to be treated equally.

There is nothing these people had that you don't have. There are thousands like them who have done extraordinary things. What they all have in common is they simply didn't allow fear to stop them from following their hearts' desires, and to imagine their dreams into being.

Are You Ready to Imagine Your Most Extraordinary Life?

Start a new relationship today with your imagination or as motivator, Napoleon Hill said, "Cherish your visions and your dreams as they are the children of your soul, the blue prints of your ultimate accomplishments." Pause to listen to those deep whisperings of your heart that are beckoning to you. The well of possibilities *within* is deep and wide.

You are equipped with everything you need to take an imaginative journey into becoming all that you want to be—a journey that holds the dreams that are yours, which are just waiting for you to bring them to life.

CHAPTER ELEVEN

The Sixth Pillar: Action

"Knowing is not enough; we must apply. Willing is not enough; we must do."
—*Johann Wolfgang von Goethe*

Here we are at the sixth pillar of transformation: action. So far, you've come to a better understanding of the workings of the mind, at all levels. You've learned about clearing the old programs that no longer serve you. You've learned the importance of setting in place the pillars of self-honesty, observation, choice, and responsibility. And now you've been coached in the power of the imagination and following the heart.

You might think of action as the time when the rubber meets the road. The precepts are there, the understanding is clear, and now it is time to get moving. I've said to audiences before, "There is a reason God made you with so many joints, muscles, and sensory apparatus. You're not made to hold still. Human beings are created for motion. To move, act, and coordinate the physical part of our being with our emotional and intellectual creativity brings us into congruence and wholeness as living, breathing earth-bound creators."

As obvious as this would seem, many of us lose sight of the importance of taking decisive, clear action as we move along in our journeys; instead wishing that everything would come together, just the way we know it could in our imaginations and hearts. But just as our hearts provide the compass to our most incredible journey, and our imaginations provide the detailed blueprint; our actions cause the blueprint to begin assembling into a living reality.

Action is *the way* we put our dreams in motion. It is the way we give our dreams a face and a presence in our physical lives. If we truly want to *live* our dreams and not simply entertain them in our imaginations, we *must* engage our whole selves in a plan of action.

Often, the pillar of action can be the most challenging one. Each of us at one time or another has become "stuck" knowing what we want, forming our best vision of it, but somehow finding ourselves without a clear course of action, nonetheless. The steps to fulfilling our dreams keep eluding us. We stay busy and yet get nowhere. There are so many areas of life that must be balanced; so many challenges that our behavior becomes repetitive and programmed. We keep putting out the fires immediately in front of us while forgetting to pick up our heads and look forward to the better things ahead. We get locked into a mundane existence of performing our necessary duties, when all the while our dreams are waiting to be channeled into actions, so that we can start living them, feeling them, and being them.

Kellie and Steve

When Kellie and Steve started coming to appointments with me they were truly stuck. Their lives had taken some unexpected turns and they found themselves in a situation neither had planned for. They had met shortly after Steve's painful and bitter divorce from his ex-wife. He had finally decided it would be okay to start dating a bit, as long as he kept things casual and took plenty of time to heal and to get to know himself again, as an individual. Kellie, a single mother with one young daughter had finally become independent from her emotionally abusive ex-husband. When she met Steve she too wanted to keep things light, as she was not ready to take on any more responsibility than she already had.

Their relationship had progressed and they'd started spending more and more time together. Eventually, one thing led to another and Kellie ended up becoming pregnant, even while on a birth control pill. Amid the conflict of duty to step up to the responsibility of bringing a child into the world and the fear of getting into something they had never deliberately decided they wanted; they moved in together to try to create a stable home environment for their new daughter and the one Kellie already had.

Shortly after they joined their households, their relationship began to deteriorate. They found themselves unable to agree on how things should flow and function—to the point that nothing in their lives was flowing or functioning. Kellie was constantly unhappy about Steve's complete non-awareness of the importance of keeping a clean, functioning household. She felt no incentive to do it herself. Because of the lack of agreement on how it should be done, she also just let it go. She started detesting her job, as an executive assistant because the long hours were such a grind and then she would come home to face a completely messy, disorganized house, two needy children, and a man whom she wasn't sure wanted to be there. She felt he was only there out of duty; not because he truly loved her and was looking forward to sharing a life with her.

Steve was completely overwhelmed by his domestic situation. He made his decision to move in with Kellie, based on the religious values he held that came from the belief that it was his duty to do so. Because of the pressure he was feeling to conform to this sudden, unplanned turn of events, he wasn't sure how he felt about his ability to love Kellie for the long term in the way she deserved to be love. His sense of overwhelm had taken him over and he was literally stuck in his tracks. The goal he had set for becoming the number one designer in their region was hanging out there in limbo. It was as if his feet, his tongue, and his mind had been dipped in thick glue. He was already one of the top designers in our city, but he couldn't seem to find the clarity of mind or purpose to get going on the jobs he had already secured, which resulted in his having a huge mounting backlog of work. On top of that he hadn't followed through the way he normally would have on new business, so his future income stream was rapidly dwindling.

Steve and Kellie were both immobilized with confusion surrounding their relationship, and the sudden, big changes they had made in their lives and from an inability to handle their conflicting emotions. If there was ever a time someone needed an action plan, this was it.

Have you heard the old saying "paralysis by analysis"? This couple was experiencing it—at its worst. Trying to analyze their emotions and the state of their relationship had paralyzed two formerly ambitious, high-functioning people into a nonfunctioning, ineffective state. At times like this there is only one way out. Stop analyzing and take action.

In the beginning of our coaching sessions they both agreed to put the relationship in a holding pattern, which meant not forcing discussion about it, giving each other space without demanding that emotional needs be met by the other, and setting healthy boundaries as to what was acceptable to each, in terms of how they interacted. Then the action could begin.

We made a detailed list of each thing that needed to be done around the house to make their home life flow and function better. This was especially important because Steve worked from a home office, and the chaos they had created had flowed right into his business, completely derailing him. The list was designed to get clutter in its place and to create systems for everyday tasks, to ensure that when any time was spent cleaning up or doing laundry, there was no effort wasted. We created the easiest, most efficient way to get household tasks done and then divided the tasks equitably between the two.

Since Steve had taken on the role as the primary breadwinner, he needed more time to focus his actions on what he did best. But Kellie also needed some "adult" time to do billing and marketing, and to deal with some of the household responsibilities without the kids in her space. Her action list started with finding a reputable day care center to take the girls for a certain number of hours a day, and getting a once-a-week helper to do deep cleaning. Her next step was to assemble a list of potential clients that would be receptive to Steve's work, and then to pick up the phone and call a few each day to try to book presentations.

The action list also called for each of them to get out of the house first thing in the morning for a half hour walk or run. They alternated days on this, so each one could get the benefits of invigorating themselves with morning exercise—giving them more energy to carry out their planned actions.

Taking action was a painstaking process at first. When they first started performing the actions, they were not wholly convinced anything would make a difference. Their efforts felt awkward and a bit disjointed, but after a couple of weeks of completing the list no matter *what*, they both conceded that life was getting easier all the time.

The boundaries were helping them get a breather from the stress about where the relationship stood, and the constructive action steps designed to make their lives more functional, made it more enjoyable and easier to be there. Since they both started accomplishing more on the career front *and* they were getting weekly exercise, they started feeling better about themselves and their self-esteem rose quickly. As I write this book they are still working through the relationship to decide if they would be better off living together or separately; but since the implementation of their action plan, they each feel more empowered, prepared, and capable of accepting the outcome and going forward to make the most of their lives.

Taking action, even when it felt awkward and unnatural was the *only* way they could possibly have broken out of the funk they were in.

Time to Get Moving

In the body of philosophical work that describes the laws of nature, Sir Isaac Newton said when referring to the law of motion, "A body at rest tends to remain at rest. A body in motion tends to remain in motion." This philosophy is quite accurate and useful, when we consider our own movement in nature. Whether navigating life's predicaments or launching a new vision, action is the step we take to put our energy into motion. When we get stuck and we're not moving ahead, it is usually because our energy is fixed at the analysis stage…swirling around in our heads making us feel frustrated and helpless because it is going nowhere. When our energy becomes frozen in our heads like this, it keeps recycling the same fears and concerns of making the *wrong* move, and given enough time it will keep us from making *any* move.

Any step forward is usually better than taking no step forward. As in Steve and Kellie's case, sometimes you just need to start putting one foot in front of the other, even if they're baby steps. Any action will get things moving along. Even if every action you take doesn't end up being the ultimate perfect move, at least your ship is launched. All you need to do then is to adjust your course. The boat to your dreams will never get launched without taking action, in a consistent and deliberate way. Your biggest breaks in life come when you are already moving toward your dreams, through your actions.

The Difference Between Lucky and Unlucky—Is Action

It is natural for us to look around at those who are successful in the areas of life we all wish to master and think, "I wish I could be so lucky." This is a little fallacy that we've become very good at entertaining in our minds. We tell ourselves we've been a bit *un*lucky at times, which explains why our lives are not all we would want them to be. We long for providence to be as kind to us as she has been to those who are obviously living the good life.

Here's the truth. We are all in the same river of life. Every day new opportunities in the form of people, resources, and ideas flow past each one of us. The *only* difference, between the people who seem to have it all and those who don't, is the first group's ability to reach out and grab onto opportunities that glide by. People who consider themselves to be unlucky, generally don't form the mental connection between their ability to act upon small opportunities and how that action, subsequently, will translate into success stories in their lives.

The Monster That Immobilizes Us

Often we begin to get a clear vision of something wonderful. We start to imagine what it would be like to live a certain way and to make these dreams a reality. Then a little creature creeps into our awareness unnoticed, at first, and sometimes unacknowledged by us. Like a goblin hiding under the bed; he remains unseen. We try to ignore him but the terror within us starts to rise. He is none other than the monster called Fear of Failure. We've all experienced his unwanted presence before… taunting us… laughing at us for even imagining we could do such grand things. His threats come in different phrases like "Who do you think you are? Why would you even try? What makes you think you have what it takes?"

The funny thing is, failure itself is not the monster. The monster lives only inside the fear. The failures we experience actually bring about the most powerful lessons we can learn. Like our most competent teachers in the classroom of life, our failures demand that we immerse ourselves in the learning, so that it can never be lost.

As author J.K. Rowling pointed out in her recent speech to graduating students at Harvard University's commencement exercises: living too cautiously prevents us from taking the actions that allow us to truly live. She discussed what she called the *benefits of failure* saying, "It is impossible to live without failing at something, unless you live so cautiously that you might as well not have lived at all, in which case, you fail by default." Don't fall into this trap.

Taking Action on the Long and Winding Road

The way before us is not necessarily a straight, paved pathway. More often than not, life unwinds ahead of us more like an obstacle course. It somehow makes it easier if we accept that within our lifetime we will encounter hills and hurdles, mud bogs and quicksand, ravines and even enormous mountains. If you approach life believing it will be a cakewalk, the discovery that it's not could leave you discouraged and overwhelmed. Instead, if you reach out to life knowing that its very purpose is inherent in its challenges, each time you make it over one of the hurdles; you will feel that much stronger. Every time you go through a ravine and come out the other side, you will feel more confident in your ability to find your way. And if the time comes when you must climb a very large mountain, which looms in front of you because there is no way around it, when you finally reach the summit—you will *know* that you are unstoppable.

Action takes courage because it requires us to keep moving through our fears and difficulties. Failing to take action, as we move through the course of life, is to let ourselves miss out on the greatest potentials that are simply awaiting our involvement. It is a given that the people in our lives will let us down at times. The most important question to ask is, "Will I let myself down by failing to act on my own behalf?"

Great Strategies for Taking Action

It's time to get your life moving! Here are some simple but powerful strategies to start putting your energy into motion.

- Make a vision board of the things you want in your life. Include magazine photos of cars, houses, pets, happy relationships, travel, successful businessmen or women, and people in careers you could see yourself doing. You can also include names of service organizations you want to be a part of, or philanthropic causes you would like to lead. Create this visual representation of what you want, and hang it in the place where you spend the most time during the day. Seeing your vision daily prompts more focused action. For a free report on how to create the ultimate vision-board go to: **www.crystaldwyer.com/vision-board.html**.

- Start by writing down your goals. Goal writing may seem like an outmoded idea to you, but your goals will provide you with a target toward which to direct your actions. If you haven't decided what you want how will you know what actions to take and what opportunities to act upon? Do a minimum of monthly goals, yearly goals, and five-year goals. Then, each Friday or Sunday write down your short-term goals for the upcoming week.

- Write down your daily action list the night before. Prioritize the actions from top to bottom.

- Start each day by looking at your action list, and imagine yourself finishing each task on it. Start moving through the action list in the morning, before you become distracted by anything else. If you have to go to work, first thing in the morning, put your job down on your list as your first action, and line the other actions up according to the times you can fit them in.

- Action steps happen more effortlessly if you are more detailed in the planning. Write detailed steps down like: "Get online/look up six life coaches" rather than "Find a life coach."

- Start with a realistic number of tasks and learn to pace yourself. No more than five.

- If there is anything undone on your list put it at the top of the list the next day.

- Action perpetuates itself and becomes a habit. No matter how much you do not feel like doing something at first, as you've heard it said—just do it. Your momentum will grow.

- Don't wait to feel motivated. Taking action will always help kick up your motivation.

- The idea is to keep moving. Don't let yourself feel overwhelmed by thinking there are too many steps between here and where you want to be. The smallest things sometimes make the biggest difference. Keep taking steps you need to take even if they feel like baby steps.

- Keep moving and moving and moving again. Deliberate contemplation or meditation to create a plan is helpful, but don't ever allow yourself just to hang in a state of limbo. Your next step may prove to be imperfect, but it will lead you to improve on the following one.

Your Actions Will Define Your Accomplishments

Think about every single thing you *have* accomplished in your life, up until now. The things you brought to fruition, the things you were recognized for, and your greatest achievements all happened *because* you took action.

Even the best-laid plans will never be without action. Our visions, and dreams imagined are the seeds of our reality. Action is the planting, watering, and pruning required to grow our most beautiful garden.

Chapter Twelve
The Seventh Pillar: Silence

"See how nature—trees, flowers, grass—grows in silence; see the stars, the moon and the sun, how they move in silence... we need silence to be able to touch souls."
—*Mother Teresa*

We've made it to the seventh and final pillar of our life transformation: silence. One reason I saved this one for last is because it is my favorite. The primary reason, however, is that when understood and experienced, silence is by far the most powerful of all of the pillars. Even as I begin to write this chapter, I feel a deep desire to communicate the depth and breadth of it, so that it will ignite a spark of recognition within you... of the presence of something beyond you... yet, as familiar as looking in the mirror.

So, what do I mean by silence? How could participating in something so notably benign activate seismic changes within our lives?

The silence I am referring to is a state that is achieved through the practice of meditation. Meditation has grown to be in vogue these days. Hollywood is meditating, college co-eds are forming meditation groups, and people ranging from country singers to dentists are leaving their homes for a month at a time, or more, to visit ashrams in India to meditate with gurus. All, so they might discover what can happen when they participate in concentrated doses of this thing called silence.

Fifteen years ago, you would have had a hard time convincing me that I would ever enjoy sitting quietly for thirty minutes, or more, at a time doing nothing and thinking nothing. I was a girl who was raised to *do*. My parents both came from a pioneering philosophy that holds: there is nothing better than a full day's work and there's always work to be done.

Whether by genetics or upbringing, or some of each, the personal philosophy I operated by basically called for me to always be in motion, even if it was only my hand moving a pen across the page, addressing bills, making punch lists, or filling out forms. I had grown up watching my mother efficiently corral nine children throughout the day, make sure they were all fed and healthy, see that massive piles of laundry were done each week, oversee our schoolwork, and get us to the right dance classes, football practices, and to bed on time. In her spare time she created little hobbies for herself—like growing massive organic gardens that we were all required to help her weed and harvest.

Then there was her sewing hobby. She thought it somehow enjoyable to cut patterns and cloth, pin all the parts together so they were right side up, and then spend hours pushing the fabric in straight lines under the pounding needle of her top-of-the-line sewing machine. This was one hobby that didn't rub off on me. My elder sister would diligently sit assembling new dresses. After the first time the thread snapped and that miniscule needle eye wouldn't accept that fat piece of thread I was trying to stuff in; I would excuse myself to go to the restroom, and sneak out to the trampoline to jump away my frustration at the "insanity" of sewing your own clothes, when you have enough money to go buy them.

In my family, the bottom line is that we all learned to work and when that work was done to look for more work to do—and call it a hobby. A girl raised like this does not immediately see the pleasure or virtue in sitting and doing, as I said... nothing.

What led me to find the joy in silence was *pain*. Isn't that how life is sometimes? The worst experiences often lead you to the best gifts. My pain started like this:

I got a call one day saying my son was in jail for possession of marijuana. It turns out it wasn't just a little bit of marijuana. My son, who possessed natural entrepreneurial skills and a youthful naiveté, had decided that since he and all of his college friends and housemates were buying the same thing—why not look for a direct distributor and buy in bulk? Somehow it never occurred to him that this type of activity is called "dealing drugs." Since he was the guy foolish enough to coordinate the direct transaction, he took the entire rap.

During the next year of my life, much of my time was spent helping him get out of the mess he was in. The State of Utah, where he was attending college has laws that make it very difficult on those who violate them. The one that says if you possess or use drugs in a drug-free zone, your original charge will be raised to one higher level—caused terror in our hearts. My son's attorney said because there were so many churches in this town—he had mapped it out and discovered there was not one block in the entire city that was *not* a drug-free zone—it meant that my son's misdemeanor was being raised by the prosecutor to the charge of a felony.

My son became a mental wreck. Court dates, filings, and hearings went on for months. I never knew what night he might call me in a full-blown panic attack feeling like he was going to die. I often would sit for hours on the phone with him to get him through the night. He was out on bail, but couldn't leave the state. Even though I would visit him often, I had two little girls at home who also needed me there. I felt torn because I couldn't be in both places at once.

All of this was happening to my beautiful boy, who I remembered had been the guy who coached his friends *against* using drugs throughout his high school years. What do you suppose happens inside a mother's body when she starts to imagine that her handsome, tall teenage son could end up serving prison time with violent adult criminals who have a reputation for preying on young, handsome, naïve prisoners? Or when she is in constant fear that the bright future we had all dreamed of and worked so hard for, could evaporate with one tragic event?

I can tell you what happened inside of my body. My anxiety rose to the point that my chemistry was so out of balance that I stopped sleeping at night. I'd lie there and think that if I could just get out of bed and run to California and back, I might be tired enough to sleep. Instead, I would stay… longing for some rest but feeling my heart beating as fast as it would, if I *were* in a dead run.

My medical doctor put me on beta-blockers to try to slow down my heart rate. Taking them made me feel like a poisoned animal always heading for water. I threw them away and went to my naturopathic physician. When he tested the chemicals in my brain, he found that the anxiety neurotransmitters were extremely high. He put me on amino acids to help rebalance the chemicals in my brain and body. After a week or so, they started to help and I began sleeping again, but as he monitored my still out-of-whack, anxiety-laden chemistry each week—he kept gently suggesting that I needed to find additional ways to reduce the stress in my life.

Eventually, the charges against my son were reduced, and he ended up serving a work/school release sentence in jail for one week, essentially checking in to go to sleep at night. The lessons he learned have been invaluable to him. He has told me that the fact that he survived unscathed, but so much wiser and more humble, made them worth it. Through the process of spending hours coaching my son to an understanding of how some of his flawed beliefs had caused this terrifying event to happen in his life, he and I became closer than we ever had been. He came to understand the power of his own choices: taking responsibility (as an adult now) for his role in what had happened and how to use his knowledge and experience to create the life he wanted.

In the few weeks following the conclusion of our year-long drama, I finally had time to think about my own life and health. The vulnerability you feel when you are threatened by something that could be devastating to the well-being and the future of someone you love… causes you to search for deeper meaning in your life. I knew something in me had changed through this experience. I wasn't sure what, but I felt something calling me into reflection… an undeniable beckoning from inside that kept telling me there was a place, *within,* I had never gone before. It was time. I knew I needed to get away from my family responsibilities, and go to a place that would allow me to gather the fragmented pieces of myself again, so that I could move past the trauma of the prior year.

I woke up one morning and suddenly thought about the beauty and simplicity of a Deepak Chopra book I had read years before, called *The Seven Spiritual Laws of Success*. I decided to look up meditation retreats at the Chopra Center for Wellbeing in California. I really didn't even know they *had* meditation retreats when I first entertained the thought, but after visiting the Chopra website I discovered they *did*. I booked myself for one that would be a week long. From the moment I booked it, I knew my healing had begun.

I flew to California for the retreat a few weeks later. It was exactly what my frazzled mind and body were craving. I sat each day with several hundred people while two brilliant, spiritual men, Deepak Chopra, M.D. and David Simon, M.D. would alternately impart their wisdom to my thirsty mind and soul. We learned a different thread of wisdom each day, and would sit for an hour each morning and an hour each afternoon, practicing and integrating the new thread every time we meditated. It was cleansing, relaxing, and a joy to be doing it with others who had a desire, as I did, to achieve peace and awareness. I could feel my nerves slowly unravel with each passing day there.

Halfway through the week, as Dr. Simon was wrapping up his final comments, he left us with the suggestion that we participate in *silence* the following day. My first thought was "Isn't that what we've been doing *every* day?" He then explained that their *suggestion* to all, halfway through each mediation course, was to encourage attendees to participate in an *entire day* of silence...as in not saying anything to anyone and not making phone calls or turning on the TV in our rooms. If we chose to participate, we would simply write "silence" on the reverse side of our nametag and wear it around all day, so that others would know not to converse or socialize with us. They asked that even when we were to eat our meals on that day, which by the way, were a buffet of healthful, delicious, vegetarian dishes; we would sit and eat quietly even if we'd chosen not to participate in the silence exercise. Thereby, we would be allowing those who had chosen silence to experience the full benefit.

My first reaction was to think they might just be taking this a little far. After all, one of the things we were all enjoying was to chatter with our newfound friends about how much we were getting from our experience, and all of the ways it would help us in our lives. As much as I was onboard with sitting quietly for a couple of hours each day, why would any of us want to deprive ourselves of the opportunity to let such nice people get to know us better? I firmly decided a full day of silence served absolutely *no* purpose in my life, and I would not be joining in the next day. I would find other sane people to socialize with and continue to enjoy my week.

The next morning, as I prepared to leave my hotel room to go down to the conference, I reached for the door handle and clearly heard a voice in my head say "Turn your nametag around and write silence." Now this was a voice that I knew didn't come from me or any alter ego I had because all of us, to that point, were in solid agreement that silence was out of the question for us. There is only one thing to do when you hear a voice that sounds so much wiser than yours telling you, in no uncertain terms, what to do. Before I could even think about it, I was closing my door, finding a pen, and writing "silence" on my nametag. My only thought as I exited my room was "Okay, I guess I'll find out what this is all about."

Something really interesting happens when you don't have your mouth working full-time spinning your ego's finest tale. It didn't take me very long that day, to realize how much I relied on the things I said to persuade the rest of the world that I was worth their time. There's only one person left to really get to know when everyone else is off limits. That person is you. When I was left to be just with myself (to get to know myself) I realized how carefully I had avoided facing the hidden parts of me. Before this day, I had only allowed myself to crack the door and peek inside; quickly shutting it when I couldn't deal with the things that might cause me discontent, or make me feel something I wasn't ready to feel. This time there was *only* me there, with the door wide open and only one way to look, which was inside myself.

Throughout the day, I could feel my emotions building like a volcano coming back to life. This day there was no way out. No clever escape route. No way to distract myself with a conversation about the high points of my hypnosis practice, or how I think the room might be just a bit warm. I couldn't even turn to the nice lady next to me and tell her how good she looked in blue. I was completely exposed to all things tucked away inside of me: the hurt, shame, guilt, unworthiness, and the fears that had consistently driven me to please those, whose love I desired, so that I could feel worthy of their love and fulfill my need to feel my presence being validated.

Toward the end of the day, Dr. Simon began reading some of the beautiful words of the Sufi poet Rumi. I heard him say something about the entire shining city of Brahman (God) being in your heart… and it finally happened. The volcano exploded as an epiphany in my heart and soul. Like stars bursting with radiance in every cell of my being… I suddenly understood the most important truth that still guides me to this day. I knew instantly, that while for much of my life I had been desperately searching for validation and the purpose of my existence everywhere outside myself; it was already inside of me. Everything I am, and everything I could become was all right there… shining like a great, limitless treasure.

Now, I hate to cry in front of people. This is something that has never been easy for me. I don't like for people to see me so vulnerable. I've never been comfortable falling apart publicly. I'm much more of a private griever. But none of those rules mattered, in that moment, because the volcano of feeling couldn't be stopped. As the light burst through me, I was so overcome with intense emotion I began shaking to try to control and subdue it a bit. My attempts were useless. This was something beyond my control. I had to let go and as I wept openly in the quiet room, simultaneously releasing my grief and seizing my newfound joy, I began to notice how others around me began to weep. I didn't know if my weeping triggered an emotional release in them, but what I hoped for them was they had experienced the same explosion of truth and light that I had.

My final tears were ones of tremendous gratitude. In those moments it was so apparent to me how God generously pours out *everything* you need… when you need it; if you only stay open to it and remain aware of it. I thanked Him for His unwavering constancy in pointing me in the right direction, even when I would like to think I have a better idea. I knew what I just learned was *truly* the secret to life.

When we feel human vulnerability, we naturally want to project out to the other living beings around us. We often tack the course we sail, according to the direction of another person, whether or not they know where they're going. The validation and sensory output we get from others, often gives us enough feedback to temporarily assuage our minds and hearts.

Looking outside ourselves for our true purpose and greatest potential only serves to pull us off our center, and reinforce the feeling that something is out of balance. The secret to deep, lasting success and happiness lies fully inside our *own* heart and soul, and can be experienced through the pillar of *silence*. Devoid of the clutter of thoughts and emotions, the place of *silence* within is our resting place for truth, light, and stability.

Before I left the Chopra Center that week, I enrolled in the teacher's certification path. I was so profoundly changed by my experience that I wanted to learn more and share what I had learned with others. Just over a year later, I officially became certified as a Chopra meditation instructor.

Meditation? How? I can't stop thinking

"Meditation is not a way of making your mind quiet. It is a way of entering into the quiet that is already there, buried under the 50,000 thoughts the average person thinks every day," says Deepak Chopra.

In my experience with helping people, the idea of being able to find a quiet, peaceful space inside ourselves sounds like something too good to be true; a place we all long to go to but aren't quite sure how to get there.

One of the most frequently asked questions I hear is: "How do I stop thinking so that I can experience silence? I can't seem to shut down my thoughts." A bit ironic isn't it—that one of the most difficult things for any of us to do is to do *nothing*? The emphasis here is on the doing. We are so entrained in our modern-day mortal existence to do, do, do that it is difficult just to *be*.

Meditation is simply about *being*. This is one of the main reasons meditation has such pronounced benefits to our health and well-being. When you release any and every expectation you have for yourself or that someone else has for you, and you just let yourself *be* for even a half an hour per day... the peace and serenity your body and nervous system experience will add years to your life.

Here are five simple steps to achieve a clear, relaxed state of silence:

1. Choose a quiet space in which you can regularly meditate. It doesn't have to be an entire room. You can play soft music or light a candle. Whatever gets you in a relaxed mood is fine. If you meditate outdoors make sure it is not in direct sunlight or an unpleasant temperature.

2. Sit comfortably. If you aren't comfortable sitting on the floor, with your legs crossed, sitting in a chair with your feet on the floor is perfectly fine. Sit with a straight spine, your head even and your eyes closed.

3. Begin with three deep, cleansing breaths, breathing all the way down to the base of the spine. Breathe in through your nose and out through your mouth. After the three deep breaths begin breathing normally again, with no effort.

4. Start to let go of all thoughts by focusing on the inflow and outflow of the breath or by repeating, silently, a simple mantra over and over. The mantra can be something like: "I am healed," "I am whole," or "I am peace." When a thought pops into your head put your attention back on your breath or your mantra. Make sure you don't focus on the meaning of the mantra because that becomes a thought. Simply use the mantra for the sound vibration. Repetition of words will draw you away from thinking and into silence.

5. Try to practice meditation, regularly. Twice a day is very beneficial: once in the morning and once again in the late afternoon or evening. A half hour to a full hour is ideal, but even if you can only work in fifteen minutes per meditation, you will still enjoy wonderful benefits.

In meditative circles, what is experienced in silence is often called such things as the gap, the zone, or the great void. None of these descriptions accurately describes the experience I have when I enter silence, especially the last one. Even though the silence I experience is devoid of mind clutter, I am fully aware of the unlimited, unbounded potential of everything I am and everything that is. I might best describe it as diving into a vast ocean of calm, pure awareness. I am a drop of water merging into the boundless sea. The perceived boundary of the drop being separate from the ocean disappears. What is experienced is oneness with God and all of creation.

If you consistently practice the pillar of silence in your life, it will become your greatest resource. You will begin to connect with an unlimited supply of solutions, ideas, and possibilities, when you dip into the silence. It will be like you are plugging into the source because that is exactly what happens, when you achieve the pureness of silence.

In the state of silence, your problems don't disappear, but they do fall easily into perspective. Often, our problems are like a pimple that seems enormous as we stare at it in the mirror from two inches away.

In silence our focus broadens to an expansive awareness of everything. Instead of seeing just an enormous, looming pimple, we see the whole face: the smile, the eyes, and lots of clear skin around the pimple. We realize that the problem is not as big as we thought it was. It's just a pimple. When you release your problems into silence, you will begin to notice that somehow, the unlimited supply of universal intelligence (you become immersed in) provides solutions without great strain or effort on your part.

When we are constantly immersed in the noise and chaos of the world, we might tell ourselves we are accomplishing more, but we are truly cutting ourselves off from our most powerful source of support. It is within *silence* that we experience God to the fullest degree possible. It is within this still place of the silence that immense shifts in our being take place.

You will be astounded by the tremendous benefits that manifest in your life, compared to the relatively small amount of time that it takes to practice meditative silence. If you are dedicated to your meditation practice, *nothing* else will bring about such noticeable changes in your health, well-being, and success.

My wish and prayer for everyone is that they will discover the incomparable experience of pure being, through the seventh transformational pillar of silence.

PART THREE

Your New Creation Begins

༺❦༻

When something isn't working, often it's necessary to go back to square one to find out why. One of the objectives I had for this book is to take you back to the origin of your *messy thinking*, which was covered in Part One, and then to move step-by-step through the Seven Pillars of Transformation (Part Two) to integrate the principles and habits that serve to help you clean up your thinking processes. The reason: When we can formulate thoughts and reconcile our emotions within our thinking process, we start to develop a consciousness with a pureness of purpose. We are then ready to attract the things we really want in our lives.

After cleaning your mental closets (so to speak) through this makeover process, the law of attraction can begin to serve the purpose you originally hoped it would, which is to assist you in drawing in the qualities, details, and scenarios of the life you *want* to be living. Here in Part Three, we are discussing how the integration of these principles within the Seven Pillars allows us to move into the universal realms and interface with the laws of karma and quantum physics—to become more deliberate in creating the life we want.

CHAPTER THIRTEEN

Karma: The Reckoning Force of All Intention

"The life I touch for good or ill will touch another life and that in turn another, until who knows where the trembling stops or in what far place my touch will be felt."
—Frederick Buechner

I write this chapter, not to impose any particular religious doctrine or beliefs on you, but to create an awareness of the inherent power of your own intentions and actions. I would be remiss if I left this out of our life transformation manual. I include it, in the interest of helping you avoid overlooking something that could possibly be highly impactful on your life experience concerning the past, present, and future. As with all of the concepts, strategies, and teachings in this book, I ultimately turn over the responsibility to you to choose what to implement or integrate into your own daily life.

By its simplest definition, karma is known as the universal law of cause and effect. The word karma has become practically a household term in recent years. Philanthropists entertain the concept of karma as they give of themselves. Karma has now found its way into our television programming as the main character, Earl in the sitcom "My Name is Earl" goes back each week in a humorous attempt to right his wrongs. My teenagers even pop off to me about what kind of karma I'm causing if they don't agree with a decision I'm making. "That's bad karma, Mom!" I wonder what my great-grandmother would have made of all of this karma talk because it certainly wasn't around during her lifetime.

Our world *is* changing, and I happen to believe that the changes are definitely for the better. In spite of the challenges we face as humankind, I believe we are becoming more evolved and more aware in our role as custodians of our future.

Awareness is what karma is all about. Imagine what chaos we could get ourselves into, as human beings, if we had no awareness that our intentions and actions have a cause and effect dynamic. If the concept of cause and effect wasn't at least vaguely present within us, we might be running helter-skelter acting on any impulse or whim, and creating havoc with our world and each other.

Karma is a Sanskrit word meaning, "act" "action" or "performance," which also encompasses each act's inherent effect. Even though karma is the most popularized word for it, most major religious or wisdom traditions have teachings that also impart this concept: that intentions and deeds carry a certain effect that is congruent with that deed or intention. The theme is present in the Christian, Jewish, Buddhist, Islam, Hindu, Sikh, and Jain philosophies. They vary a bit on how they express the idea, but the underlying idea is that the meaning of one's thoughts, words, and actions carry a residue that affects a person's life experience or salvation. In the Bible, for instance, Jesus says, "Whatsoever a man soweth, that shall he also reap."

Understanding the Energy of Intention

Years ago, I read a book by David Hawkins, M.D., Ph.D. called *Power vs. Force* (Hay House, 2002). In it he brings a scientific basis to the karmic concept. I could go on and on about the brilliance of this man, the monumental work he has done, and the wisdom he imparts through this book, but I won't. The essence of his message is the nature of causality. He contends that human consciousness has proceeded slowly because we look to correct *effects* of our problems, rather than their causes. And he says that the *causes exist* within our consciousness inside our minds.

Using the science of kinesiology, Dr. Hawkins elaborated on the previous work of John Diamond, M.D., in which a person's muscle response is used to calibrate positive or negative stimuli to determine the energetic or spiritual quality, if you will, of everything from virtues, art, and language to toxic substances. He made the distinction that things positive in nature correspond with the qualities of power, and things negative in nature correspond with the energy of force. Power is constructive. It has the ability to ennoble, sustain, uplift, and expand. Force is destructive. It has the ability to polarize, deplete, destroy, and divide. The book includes a comprehensive list of the power and force patterns of human attitudes, which I recommend that everyone study.

It's fascinating to read about science as it is coupled with Hawkins' profound spiritual journey. Science aside, all human beings have a natural intuition that dwells within about the reality of karmic balance. We naturally feel better when we take the high road, when we act from love rather than fear or anger, and when we consider the greater good in each of our choices. When we stand in loving, truthful power, all good things are drawn toward us because we are loving, stable, and constant. With force there is always a counterforce. When we try to force our will through intimidation, fear, or manipulation, we attract back to us the very qualities and the force through which they were exercised. This is what the book, *The Secret* (Atria Books/Beyond Words, 2006), teaches: It is most powerful to embody and be all of the things you desire to attract. When you *are* the qualities and characteristics you desire, you become a magnet for all good things.

I believe the truth of karma to be this: The Universe is a perfect accounting system. Every single choice you make contributes to who you are and what you do, and it gets woven into the universal fabric. The energy of all of your thoughts, words, and deeds not only determines where you are in this vast universal field; it also influences the quantum energetic field itself.

It's therefore good to notice where you are. Then ask yourself where you want to be. Karma is the fruit of your deeds and intentions.

What if we were to consistently consider the influence of our thoughts and actions on our entire world? In Judaism, karmic law exists in the concept of *teshuva*. Teshuva holds that, collectively, we all have it within our power to stop human suffering. In the midst of human suffering *anywhere*, we must each examine our own deeds to determine our contribution to the tragedy, even if it is a huge disaster.

What Goes Around Comes Around

Yes, we've all heard it said before. The energy of your actions, thoughts, words, and intentions will indeed come around to you, again and again. This includes *everything*.

Deepak Chopra often says that even drinking a cup of coffee creates karma. That's not to say it's good or bad. It just is. In fact, you might view your coffee drinking in this way: You contributed to the coffee farmers and their families in Columbia, and you created a more acidic environment in your stomach (and according to recent studies) you may be preventing colon cancer and cleansing your liver. However, if the coffee wasn't organic, you also might have contributed to the pesticides in the environment.

Obviously, some actions are more benign than others and their numerous effects might neutralize each other in the karmic picture. The point is that there are no extraneous choices for you to make. They are all included in the grand scenery. *Nothing* you do exists in a void. Thus, each of us is responsible for our own lives as well as for the possible pain or joy we could create in the lives of others.

As you develop awareness, you will begin to notice the energetic quality of what returns to you in the form of your reality. Awareness brings about the virtue of discernment. Discernment is considered to be a highly spiritual quality. Discernment differs from judgment, in that it seeks only to understand the energetic quality inherent in something. Unlike judgment it is not righteous or punishing.

Obviously, our discernment abilities develop with time, age, and experience. There is a factor of deliberate knowing and understanding *meaning* within the karmic energy field. If a two-year-old steals cookies and lies about it, his lack of consequential understanding prevents him from doing it out of maliciousness. The reverberation of karmic energy is completely different than it would be if a thirty-two year old man steals money from his sister's wallet. The meaning and context of the act is what determines the energy that is attracted back to the person involved in the act.

Every day when we wake up, we have another whole day of opportunity in front of us to create either heaven or hell in our lives, depending on the quality of our intentions and actions. Give yourself a little reminder of this wonderful chance given to you, each day, to renew the direction of your life in the present and future. You own your karma. Go make that a wondrous gift.

CHAPTER FOURTEEN

Quantum Leaps: Implementing the Pillars for Massive Change

"Find thoughts that are good because it is inevitable that you are always going to be moving toward something. So why not be moving toward something that is pleasing?"
—*Abraham-Hicks*

※

Even the idea of discussing the subject of quantum physics is exciting to me. The study of quantum physics is the closest thing to a quantifiable explanation of the partnership we have with our infinite universe, which gives us our ability to co-create the reality we live in.

If you look around, you will see people all over the world searching for and embracing deeper realms of understanding of the nature and meaning of life. Through such ideas as conscious creating and the law of attraction, the principles of quantum physics are now present in mainstream media. They are showing up in blockbuster movies and bestselling books. In these cinematic and literary works, the reality behind the spiritual concept (known as the law of attraction) is often extolled for its unequaled power in shaping what we know as life. Quantum physics delves deeply into the fabric of our reality to explain how the micro-universe affects the macro-universe... helping us to understand the quantifiable forces that govern our universe.

In this chapter, my goal is to integrate an understanding of quantum physics, the nature of reality, and the law of attraction into our work with the Seven Pillars of Transformation. These are our foundation for taking quantum leaps. Integrating this understanding into your daily life will increase your ability to bring about transformations that seem miraculous and magical.

Me, Dad, and the Law of Attraction

I feel very blessed to have grown up the way I did. Despite some of the challenges my family experienced, I was fortunate to have two parents who had an unflappable belief that anything could be accomplished through positive, clear thinking. As I got older and began to study the world's wisdom traditions, I finally understood the role my father played in inculcating in me the precepts of the law of attraction, which would become integral to my personal philosophy.

I remember, at age 15 riding along in the front seat of my dad's Cadillac. My older sister was asleep in the back seat. Dad had decided we needed some father/daughter bonding time, so he and a business partner had booked a week-long rafting trip down the Colorado River; both dads bringing their two eldest daughters along for the fun. As we were driving along listening to some music on our eight-track player, my dad reached for the button, turned down the music, and began to talk about life—more specifically about my life: who I am and who I *think* I am. This was not the first time my dad had raised this particular topic with me. In fact, I remember thinking "Oh gosh, here he goes again with all of this deep universal-God stuff."

I was half listening for the first few minutes, still trying to clear my head from thoughts of the boyfriend I had just left behind, for a week, and all of the fun things my friends might be participating in during my absence. As he talked on, somewhere in the middle of my selfish teenage-ness, I realized that Dad was being earnest in his attempt to share his knowledge with me. It dawned on me that this really meant *something big* to him, so perhaps I should try to tune in more. At the point I tuned in, he said something I will always remember. He told me that although people often think of God as a big man in the sky who is there to decide if you are good or bad, that is not the truth. He said that God is actually much bigger and grander than any man; so big and grand in fact, that His greatness can't be held in what we think of as a body.

Then, Dad said something that changed everything for me forever. He said, "That is how God can be everywhere and in everything." He went on to say that because God can be everywhere and in everything, He also is in me. Because of that, everything that I want to be—I can be. I just need to believe I already am what I want to be. Suddenly that made such good sense to me. How could God, the big man be everywhere and in everything? It didn't seem possible. I realized to be in His greatness, God must also be boundless and His boundlessness makes anything possible. This good news felt perfectly right in my heart and mind. It was my first learning about the universal law of attraction.

First of All, What *Is* Quantum Physics?

Quantum physics studies the behavior of all matter and energy—molecular, atomic, and nuclear—at the most microscopic levels. Since the world we "see" each day, including our bodies, is *all* matter made up of energy, it's important to understand what is causing the matter and energy that exists in your life to exist in its current form. An atom is really the smallest particle we can still call "matter." The smaller parts that make up the atom, the protons, electrons, and neutrons, and the even smaller units that compose them, such as quarks are nothing more than units of energy.

It was discovered in the early twentieth century, that the laws and mathematical formulas of traditional physics don't apply when calculating the behavior of subatomic units of energy. Contrary to those models of an atom (that those of us over the age of forty were shown in our middle school science classes) electrons don't circulate around the nucleus of an atom like planets in orbit. Electrons are nothing more than clouds of probability that randomly burst in and out of existence. In fact, most of what we think of as an atom is energy and empty space. So this energy and empty space that we call an atom is what makes up all matter, which is what we think of as the "real" world!

Throughout the twentieth century, notable scientists such as Max Planck, Albert Einstein, Niels Bohr, and Erwin Schrödinger played key roles in developing the quantum physical theories we know today. Interestingly, even though there are competing interpretations of quantum physics within the science community, each one accounts for all of the facts and anticipates its experiments' outcomes accurately. I won't get into all of the variations of quantum theories at their most mind-boggling reaches. Here, it is important to understand the most fundamental concepts of the field of quantum physics, including the Heisenberg Uncertainty Principle, which I will discuss now.

We talked about subatomic units as energy. Unlike smooth waves with gentle undulations (which is how you might imagine sound waves would move) subatomic units are known as wave packets. They are like tight bursts of concentrated energy with sharp peaks and troughs. These wave packets can either behave like a particle or like a wave. A wave packet actually becomes either a particle *or* a wave depending on whether you, the observer, inquire about its location or its movement. If the question is, "Where is it?" it will be observed as a particle. If the question is "What is its movement?" it will be observed as a wave.

Within this phenomenon of wave-particle duality, we find particles acting like waves and waves acting like particles. Physicists believe that it is the conscious observation of the wave-particle that causes it to *collapse* into either a wave or a particle.

A particularly well-known experiment, originally done in 1801, by a young English physicist named Thomas Young proved the wave-particle theory.[1] In this "double-slit" experiment a light source was directed through two parallel slits cut into a plate, so that the light passing through it would hit a screen behind the slotted plate. Scientists were able to observe an interference pattern, after the light passed through the slits that is typical of the *wave* nature of light. However, they always found the light absorbed by the back screen as particles called photons.

If the light was traveling as a particle to the screen, then the number of photon particles measured on the screen should have been the sum total of those that had gone through the left slit and the right slit, even if one or the other slit was blocked. Instead, they found that blocking the slit caused some points on the screen to be darker and others to be lighter; a phenomenon which can only be explained through the additive and subtractive behaviors of a *wave*, not the exclusively additive nature of a *particle*.

The experiment thus showed, that light can demonstrate both wave and particle characteristics, but not at the same time. Results are dependent on the measurement the observer is seeking. Claus Jönsson repeated the experiment in 1961 at the University of Tubingen—this time using electrons rather than light. His experiment demonstrated the same wave-particle duality with electrons, as the original did with light.

In his book, *The Spontaneous Fulfillment of Desire*, Deepak Chopra says, "Without consciousness acting as an observer and interpreter everything would exist only as pure potential."[2] In 1935 Albert Einstein was still not completely satisfied that the description of reality through quantum mechanics was complete. Einstein, along with his two assistants, Boris Podolsky and Nathan Rosen set up an experiment on thought. The experiment questioned what would happen if we sent two identical wave-particles off in opposite directions. Since the particles were identical, whatever measurement calculation was formulated for one would hold true for the other one, by definition. When you know the location of wave particle A, which causes it to collapse into a particle, you are simultaneously aware of the location of wave-particle B, also collapsing it into a particle.

This experiment, which was confirmed mathematically, proved that observing one of the identical wave-particles in a certain location instantly affects the other wave-particle, now in a different location. The experiment proved the existence of some form of *nonlocal* communication taking place between two separate wave-particles in two separate locations. The implication of this work is that there is a connection between the energy units that make up all of life—and that communication is taking place. Communication is happening constantly, and at a rate of exchange that is faster than the speed of light. The conclusion has become known as the Einstein-Podolsky-Rosen paradox.[3]

There is now sufficient experimental data in the field of quantum physics to fill volumes. Having established a scientific basis to our understanding of how life manifests itself; let's think about the implications of this body of scientific work as it pertains to our own *messy thinking*, and its potentially harmful or destructive affect on our lives.

Quantum science is showing us how our observations, thoughts, and emotions are attractors for what is showing up in our lives. The law of attraction *is* real. Quantum physics provides a scientific explanation for why it is real and why it works. However, as I mentioned in the Introduction, people have become a bit disenchanted with the concept of the law of attraction. Many have found that even after reading up on the subject, and trying to implement the idea of just thinking and believing they are everything they want to be—they are falling short of their goals. The intentions they are sharing with the universe don't seem to be heard, and consequently not much has changed in their lives.

Imagine, for a minute that you suddenly decide you are ready to run in a competitive race. You are tired of sitting around; you're a bit out of shape, but you know it's time for you to get up and get moving.

Instead of looking at yourself and taking a quick assessment of what it might take to be *ready* to run the race, you are convinced that it is such a good idea that your enthusiasm, alone, will get you through. So you enter and start running with all of your might. Well, suddenly you notice that the shoes you're wearing are quite worn down, and they aren't actually made for running. Then your feet begin to ache. Then you realize that your knees are throbbing, and you begin to feel the painful impact of every single step you take. After a while, you feel yourself losing stamina fast, and the race is only one-third over. And then you start to grasp the understanding that despite your enthusiasm, this isn't working out the way you expected it to. This metaphor describes the feelings of defeat that some people experience, when they started counting on the law of attraction to solve their problems and bring them what they want.

It's very difficult to jump into the race no matter how easy or exhilarating it may seem, without knowing what we have to work with at the start. Without a discovery process of what lies in the depths of our subconscious minds, those imbedded programs, filters, and beliefs are still fully engaged... influencing our thoughts, emotions, and what we pay attention to. That which we pay attention to, that which we think about, and that which we apply emotional energy to will continue to collapse the energy wave-particles that are around us and a part of us; thereby, creating a reality consistent with the quality of those hidden subconscious events. Our mind makeover assists us in discovering what we have to work with, and how to improve our mental and emotional condition so we are *ready* to join the race, and enjoy the exhilaration that can be felt when intentionally applying the law of attraction.

How Each of the Seven Pillars Sets up Clear Attractor Fields

Let's recap the significance of each of the Seven Pillars of Transformation and how they will influence our energy field, so that we become a beacon to the universe for the things we love.

Self-honesty: When we can honestly express our feelings and fears, especially to ourselves, we no longer have to create ego identities that are less virtuous than our authentic soul-self. Living more authentically attracts to us people, relationships, and situations that have a high level of integrity. Eventually, we begin to feel like we can depend on people more and start to operate from a deeper level of trust.

Self-honesty allows you to admit your imperfections, so that you can improve upon them. It lets you forgive yourself when you aren't perfect, which allows the universe to stop magnetizing the qualities of a phony ego that insists on being right. When you can forgive yourself, you release the urge to be harsh and critical with yourself. Self-criticism often sounds like "How could you be so stupid" and other phrases we wouldn't want to attract back to us from reality.

Honestly recognizing your good qualities and simply admitting and learning from mistakes, draws back to you the qualities you genuinely desire; thereby, drawing in people who also embody those authentic, genuine qualities. When you can be honest and forgive your imperfections, your focus switches to things that resonate with your essential soul. As you come more into alignment with your higher self, you will attract people who are in a higher level of alignment with their soul truth.

Observation: Observation is our best friend in the creation of a new life. Its job is to stop *messy thinking* in its tracks, and keep us from traversing well-worn thought pathways that potentially could lead us where we don't want to go. Observation as a constant exercise lets us stop quantum motion that goes in the wrong direction. It keeps us from recreating thoughts and emotional states at the quantum level that would attract more despair and confusion to us. When we step into our observation mode, we remove ourselves, for a moment, from automatic thoughts and emotional reactivity. In moments of pure observation infinite potential exists. The observation moment is a moment of pure potentiality.

Choice: When we are operating from a state of self-honesty, and taking important moments to observe the awareness we have about our choice of thought, word, or deed, we awaken to the power we carry in each moment. At this point, we understand the quantum reality we live in, and the importance of discerning the quality of each choice we make. Each of our choices causes an energetic shift in the quantum landscape we live in... no matter how small it may seem.

Our universe in its grand design accounts for each and every one of them. Nothing you choose to think, say, or do exists in a void. It all holds an inherent power to influence the reality of our lives. So choose deliberately, choose with discernment, and be purposeful in your choices.

Responsibility: When you step up and claim responsibility over your life, you are making exalted statements to the universe that no longer will your power belong to anyone but you. As you take back ownership of yourself and your life, millions of little units of energy will collapse into a reality that speaks of leadership, personal strength, and ingenuity. Making a daily proclamation of stewardship over yourself and your life will cause the universe to answer you, with unlimited resources and resourcefulness.

Imagination: When you really use your imagination it registers in the quantum realm—like a glorious designer of life—sculpting new scenarios, planning grand adventures, or featuring you as the grandest version of yourself. The imagination, getting its cues from the heart, dances and plays in the quantum realm... and even in its dancing and playfulness, it engages those little units of life energy into the dance and the play. Don't underestimate the power of your imagination to activate your most elaborate dreams and make them real. Imaginative energy is an enticingly powerful attractor in the quantum field.

Action: The pillar of action is essential because it involves the physical version of you... causing a deeper influence in your quantum creation. Taking action brings you into congruence with the mental, emotional, and spiritual parts of you, which will certainly make you a more harmonious attractor field. All parts of you make the whole you; so putting yourself into motion causes energy shifts throughout the quantum field around you. The only way to be fully engaged in the creation process, at the quantum level, is to physically act toward or on behalf of all of the things, people, and places that you desire to have in your life.

If you really want something to be a part of your life, you must jump into the quantum soup, regularly, to connect with the energy packets circulating throughout that already contain what it is you want. If you state your dreams and set your goals, but your physical self remains unengaged, you are actually sending a message to the universe, "I really *don't* want what I say I want." Decide what you want, get a clear imaginative vision of that, and then wake up each day and *do* as many things as you can to support that vision. The more steps you take each day in the physical world, the more you will receive feedback from that quantum realm that matches what you are going after. This process serves to hone and refine your goals, often leading you toward something even better than you imagined!

Silence: The silence pillar, when used regularly, can become the most powerful attractor in the fulfillment of your desires. Silence offers you a clear, serene space (free from mental and emotional clutter) to commune with your Creator and all of creation. With all of the other pillars set in place, you can set clear, pure intentions for all of your greatest desires and release them into the silence. In silence, when you are free from thoughts and emotions, you become an attractor field unencumbered by forces that otherwise might interfere with the pure desires of your heart.

The extent to which you can release your thinking and go into the stillness with your clearest intentions will determine how powerfully your life will begin to move in quantum leaps.

With our new transformational tools, each day we will go about our lives with a new level of consciousness about the way we are living it. An essential element of our consciousness should be gratitude for all that we have and experience. Gratitude is a powerful concept that we can both feel and practice. Noticing all that life is offering you, in each moment, affirms to the universe that you are not missing the gifts it is providing you. From a new blossom on the flower, outside your window, to the joy you see behind the crinkled eyes of an elderly person who is happy to see you... appreciating the special beauty moment-by-moment is *the way* to open the glorious floodgate to the abundance of the universe.

It is especially important to offer thanks to your Creator for the challenges that make you stronger, and the problems that cause you to turn to the resources of your internal genius. In giving thanks, you will find yourself effortlessly accessing the solutions and resolutions that drive you in becoming the next best version of you. Life is meant to *be a journey* not an end. Noticing and expressing gratitude for all experience, within the journey, becomes one of *the* most powerful attractor forces available.

Quantum physics is the mathematical explanation we give to this complex choreography between all of our words, thoughts, actions, emotions, interactions, and intentions, which all come together to create this elegant dance of life. Our personal dance then spins its way into the quantum galaxy to become a partner to the swirling, twirling movement of all humanity.

Recommended Resources

I created the following programs to assist you in cleaning up your *messy thinking*.

Pure Thoughts for Pure Results—Living the Life You Deserve *Seminar*

This seminar is available to small or large groups and can be tailored from a half day to two full days. In this seminar, I personally guide you step-by-step through the foundations of *messy thinking* and how they began. I then take you through the principles of the Seven Pillars of Transformation using lots of audience participation, live hypnosis, and EFT sessions—working on people's specific issues. People are astounded at the enormous benefits of going through this process live and working through real life stories that are universal to all of us.

The second half of the seminar is facilitated by my longtime friend and coaching partner, Daune Thompson. Daune is a certified life coach and holds a bachelors degree in kinesiology. With her extensive experience doing speaking and training for Fortune 500 companies, and her advanced training in the healing arts, Daune is the perfect partner to take you through an awakening process toward living the life you deserve.

Pure Thoughts for Pure Results *Coaching*

Imagine how your much your life will change with **two months** of in-depth coaching with Crystal! This package includes a 30-minute phone session each week with Crystal for eight weeks. Daily life will always present challenges. Spend one-on-one time with Crystal and see for yourself how her mastery in coaching and hypnosis, coupled with her keen intuition will help you through the most important or trying times.

Pure Thoughts for Pure Results *Home Kit*

This is a full program for at-home use. Like a seminar in a box it includes the step-by-step workbook that guides you through every concept in the *free-from-messy-thinking* program. Included are exercises, planning sheets, a vision-board booklet, and customized CDs in which hypnosis, NLP, and guided imagery are combined with state-of-the-art healing music. These CDs help you release old mental programs and *messy thinking,* at the subconscious level and then guide you into new mental conditioning and programs. The home kit will help you achieve mental freedom and clarity to go forward with your new life creation.

For more information on these and other programs, please visit

www.CrystalDwyer.com/Programs.

CD Hypnosis/Guided Imagery Programs to Purge Messy Thinking

To bring your life makeover into reality, it is time to purge any *messy thinking* programming that would hold you back from your greatest transformation. I created the following CD programs to do just that. Each CD provides the daily support you need to release you from specific issues, so that you can live the life of your dreams! All CDs are available from my website: **www.crystaldwyer.com/store**.

Starting Over or Any Life Change (2 CDs)
Learn to Make Life Happen for You **and** *The Garden of New Beginnings*

Learn to Make Life Happen for You is a mini-seminar in which you will learn about the way your mind and thoughts work, and the way your subconscious mind can sabotage your own success, health, or well-being. This program teaches about your ability to create your life the way YOU want, using the amazing potential of your own mind. This is the first CD in a two-part starter kit, which we recommend using before any of the other hypnotherapies.

The Garden of New Beginnings is the second CD in the Starter Set. This CD program utilizes powerful tools to help you activate new beginnings of all kinds in your life. It is designed to assist you in letting go of what isn't serving you, for good, and start you off with a clean slate for the wonderful road that lies ahead. A must-have when you are activating life change.

Getting Rid of Anxiety (1 CD)

Freedom from Anxiety

Using beautiful, peaceful guided imagery and hypnotherapy techniques, this powerful program, *Freedom from Anxiety* addresses the root causes of anxiety and assists you in releasing those. Using this program, regularly, will help you create a sense of internal peace and wellness in your life. You don't have to live with crippling anxiety any longer.

Overcoming Depression (1 CD)
Living Free of Depression

This transforming CD program, *Living Free of Depression* uses beautiful guided imagery and special hypnotherapy techniques to root out the causes of depression. It goes into all levels of the mind to retrain destructive depression cycle patterns and create lightness and positive, productive thought patterns, at each level of consciousness. You *can* live free of depression, now.

Healing the Mind-Body-Spirit (1 CD)
Healing Meditation: Healing the Body at All Levels to Achieve Perfect Health

A revolutionary approach to complete healing; this powerful healing tool addresses healing, at all levels of the body and mind, using very special hypnotherapy techniques. This CD is a must-have for everybody.

Learn to use the power of your own mind for perfect health. It is time to experience healing now.

Overcoming Insomnia (1 CD)
Overcoming Insomnia: Getting Deep, Refreshing Sleep Every Night

Make insomnia a thing of the past. This revolutionary program goes right to the heart of recurring interrupted sleep-cycle patterns and clears the problem, from all levels of the mind, for good. Don't wait. Start getting great sleep now.

Weight Loss Hypnosis (2CDs)
Weight Loss 1: Conquering the Weight Issue Forever
Weight Loss 2: The Real Me

No diet is permanently effective without this shift in consciousness happening first. The first half of the 2-part weight loss series, *Weight Loss 1: Conquering the Weight Issue Forever.* This revolutionary program utilizes the power of the mind, at all levels of consciousness to create a more harmonious environment for the cells of the body to safely increase metabolism. The technique used, also helps to create a more harmonious environment for the cells of the body to function optimally and to loose unwanted weight. It is time for a new approach to weight loss.

The second part of the weight loss series CD program, *Weight Loss 2: The Real Me* is remarkably powerful in creating a new, fit, slim mental image, at all levels of the mind, which the systems, cells, metabolism, and habits begin to respond to. This program reframes in the mind, both the habits and self-image, to that of a healthy, slim person. I believe this is the key to permanent weight loss. No diet is permanently effective, without this shift in consciousness happening first.

Rebalance Your Energy Chakra Clearing (1 CD)
The Colors of the Rainbow: Clearing and Balancing Your Chakra Energy

The seven energy centers, which run parallel to the spine, are called *chakras*. Chakra means "wheel" in Sanskrit. Understanding of the chakras came originally from the old Eastern wisdom traditions. Today, understanding is integrated into Western culture. This method has nothing to do with religion and everything to do with the energy centers that play an important role in the balance of physical, mental, and spiritual health.

This CD uses beautiful guided imagery to help you become more in tune with your own energy and assists you in balancing your chakras and centering yourself. Using this program, regularly, will help to integrate your physical, mental, and spiritual energies.

Smoking Cessation (1 CD)
Quit Smoking Now

It is time for you to no longer be a slave to the smoking/nicotine habit. This powerful CD will allow you to completely eliminate the smoking habit and to change your identity to that of a healthy, independent non-smoker forever. You will love the freedom you feel from quitting the old smoking habit and your body will love feeling healthy and clear of the toxins, allowing you to *truly* be your best. Congratulations for making this important commitment to yourself.

Recommended Books for Your Mind Makeover

Molecules of Emotion by Candace B. Pert, Ph.D. (Scribner, 1997).

The Biology of Belief by Bruce Lipton (Elite Books, 2005).

Change Your Brain, Change Your Life by Daniel G. Amen (Three Rivers Press, 1998).

Power vs. Force by David R. Hawkins, M.D., Ph.D. (Hay House, 1995).

You Can Heal Your Life by Louise Hay (Hay House, 1984).

Energy Medicine by Donna Eden (Putnam, 1998).

Spontaneous Healing by Andrew Weil, M.D. (Ballantine, 1995).

The Possible Human by Jean Houston Ph.D. (Putnam, 1982).

The Seven Spiritual Laws of Success by Deepak Chopra (Amber-Allen/New World Library, 1994).

The Power of Now by Eckhart Tolle (Namaste Publishing, 1994).

Infinite Mind by Valerie Hunt Ph.D. (Malibu Publishing, 1995).

New Age Hypnosis by Bruce Goldberg (Llewellyn Publications, 1998).

The Spontaneous Fulfillment of Desire by Deepak Chopra (Three Rivers Press, 2003).

There's a Spiritual Solution to Every Problem by Wayne Dyer (Harper Collins, 2001).

The Wisdom of Healing by David Simon M.D. (Three Rivers Press, 1997).

The Power of Focus by Jack Canfield, Mark Victor Hansen, and Les Hewitt. (Health Communications, 2000).

The One Minute Millionaire: The Enlightened Way to Wealth by Mark Victor Hansen and Robert G. Allen (Harmony Books, 2002).

Remembering Wholeness by Carol Tuttle (Elton - Wolf Publishing, 2000).

Recommended Websites and Programs for Your Mind Makeover

Emotional Freedom Technique

www.emofree.com

Gary Craig, the founder of Emotional Freedom Technique, offers a free beginning manual and free video to get you started with EFT on this website.

Science for Success

www.Scienceforsuccess.com

Doug Bench features some fabulous mind transformation courses.

Gaiam Yoga Club

www.gaiamyogaclub.com

Rodney Yee features fabulous online yoga courses for home use. These are great for keeping your body in balance, when you're short on time.

Notes

Chapter 2, You Thought You Were Your Thoughts

1. The National Science Foundation conducted a study showing that the brain processes somewhere around 60,000 thoughts per day at both the conscious and subconscious levels. This appears to have become an accepted fact, which is often cited without a listed source, by professionals in the areas of mind science or psychology.

2. Doug Bench. *Mind Your Brain,* CD program (McIntosh, FL: Science for Success Systems and Seminars). Website: **www.scienceforsuccess.com.**

Chapter 3, Anatomy of a Thought

1. Bruce Lipton, Ph.D. *The Biology of Belief* (Santa Rosa, CA: Elite Books, 2005): pp.67–9.

Chapter 5, Emotions: Your Mind/Body Connection

1. Candace B. Pert, Ph.D. *Molecules of Emotion* (New York: Scribner 1997): pp.22–7.

2. Robert Ader, Ph.D., M.D. *Psychoneuroimmunology* (Elsevier Academic Press, 2007). This particular experiment was considered to be one of the key discoveries of mind-body research. Ader's work became a fundamental building block to this entire field of PNI.

3. Ellen Langer, Ph.D., conducted a study with her student Alia Crum, which was reported in *Psychological Science* (February 6, 2007), a publication of the Association for Psychological Science. Read the full article at: **www.eurekalert.org/pub_releases/2007-02/afps-mmw020607.php**.

4. Chris Woolston. "Ills and Conditions: Depression and Heart Disease," *CVS/pharmacy Health Information Center* (posted January 12, 2000, updated January 28, 2008). The author cites several studies linking depression and the risk of heart attack, conducted at institutions that include Johns Hopkins University, Duke Medical Center, and the National Heart, Lung, and Blood Institute. Website: **www.cvshealthresources.com/topic/depheart**.

5. *Louis Schiavone, contributor.* "Depression May Lead to Cancer, Study Shows," *CNN Interactive* (posted December 15, 1998). The National Institute on Aging conducted a study, which shows the link between depression and cancer. Website: **www.cnn.com/HEALTH/9812/15/depression.cancer/index.html**.

6. Will Dunham. "Study Finds Depression Can Trigger Diabetes," *Reuters.com* (posted June 18, 2008). Researchers from Johns Hopkins University School of Medicine conducted a study, which confirmed the link between depression and the onset of diabetes. Website: **www.reuters.com/article/healthNews/idUSN1735710620080618**

7. Sloane Miller. "Asthma and Depression: Which Comes First?" *MyAsthmaCentral.com* (posted February 22, 2008). The Journal of Clinical Psychology published a study, which demonstrated that children with internalizing disorders, such as depression or anxiety, were more likely to suffer from asthma and require more medications than other children. Website: **www.healthcentral.com/asthma/c/9032/20696/asthma-depression**.

8. Chris Woolston. "Depression and High Blood Pressure" *AhealthyMe.com* (posted January 12, 2000, updated January 28, 2008). A recent study was done by the Centers for Disease Control and Prevention, which concluded that

depression and anxiety both play a major role in hypertension. Website: **www.ahealthyme.com/topic/depbp**.

9. Pert: p.190.

10. Ephraim C. Trakhtenberg. "The Effects of Guided Imagery on the Immune System: A Critical Review," *International Journal of Neuroscience*, volume 118, issue 6 (June 2008): pp. 839-55.

Chapter 14, Quantum Leaps

1. Claus Jönsson. "Electron Diffraction at Multiple Slits," *The American Journal of Physics*, volume 42, issue 1 (January 1974): pp. 4–11.

2. Deepak Chopra. *The Spontaneous Fulfillment of Desire* (New York: Three Rivers Press, 2003): p.51.

3. Albert Einstein. *Essays in Science*. Philosophical Library (1954): p. 100.

About the Author

Crystal Dwyer is a top leader in transformational life coaching. She founded her company, CrystalVision Ltd., for the purpose of creating a signature program that is bringing about monumental changes in people's lives. Using her mastery in life coaching, hypnotherapy, emotional freedom technique (EFT), and neuro-linguistic programming (NLP), she has helped thousands transform in all areas of life. Her techniques are a unique blend of science and keen spiritual intuition; a combination that brings powerful shifts to happen in the lives of those she works with.

Crystal is a sought-after speaker and author. She is president and co-founder of the Power of Wow, a partnership of women delivering seminars on self-empowerment, life transformation, and performance, to non-profits, corporations, small business associations, and women's organizations. She co-authored the book *101 Great Ways to Improve Your Life* with other personal empowerment experts including Jack Canfield, Bob Proctor, and John Gray, has published hundreds of self-help articles, has written and recorded fourteen hypnotherapy programs and is currently working on two new books to be released next year.

Crystal has master certifications in life coaching and hypnotherapy… is certified by the American Board of Hypnotherapy and has completed advanced training in EFT and NLP. She has worked for many years with non-profits that benefit women and children. She has also chaired fundraisers for educational scholarships for underprivileged children. Knowing that each of us contributes to the whole, her vision is to reach as many people as she can, and with her special knowledge and techniques, to help others become the best possible version of themselves; thereby, making the world a little bit better.

To find out more about Crystal's programs, books, or seminars, please contact her at:

CrystalVision Ltd.

4300 N. Miller Road, Suite 110-3

Scottsdale, AZ 85251

Phone: 602-343-1402

www.crystaldwyer.com

Made in the USA
Charleston, SC
08 July 2010